MARITIME HISTORY SERIES

Series Editor

John B. Hattendorf, *Naval War College*

Volumes Published in this Series

Pietro Martire d'Anghiera, et al.
The history of travayle in the West and East Indies (1577)
Introduction by Thomas R. Adams,
John Carter Brown Library

Willem Ysbrandsz. Bontekoe
Die vier und zwantzigste Schiffahrt (1648)
Introduction by Augustus J. Veenendaal, Jr.,
Instituut voor Nederlandse Geschiedenis, The Hague

Josiah Burchett
A complete history of the most remarkable transactions at sea (1720)
Introduction by John B. Hattendorf,
Naval War College

Alvise Cà da Mosto
Questa e una opera necessaria a tutti li naviga[n]ti (1490)
bound with:
Pietro Martire d'Anghiera
Libretto de tutta la navigatione de Re de Spagna (1504)
Introduction by Felipe Fernández-Armesto,
Oxford University

Martín Cortés
The arte of navigation (1561)
Introduction by D. W. Waters,
National Maritime Museum, Greenwich

John Davis
The seamans secrets (1633)
Introduction by A. N. Ryan,
University of Liverpool

Francisco Faleiro
Tratado del esphera y del arte del marear (1535)
Introduction by Onesimo Almeida,
Brown University

Gemma, Frisius
De principiis astronomiae & cosmographiae (1553)
Introduction by C. A. Davids,
University of Leiden

Tobias Gentleman
Englands way to win wealth, and to employ ships and marriners (1614)
bound with:
Robert Kayll
The trades increase (1615)
and
Dudley Digges
The defence of trade (1615)
and
Edward Sharpe
Britaines busse (1615)
Introduction by John B. Hattendorf,
Naval War College

William Hacke
A collection of original voyages (1699)
Introduction by Glyndwr Williams,
Queen Mary and Westfield College, University of London

*Marine architecture:
or Directions for carrying on a ship from the first laying of the keel
to her actual going to sea* (1739)
Introduction by Brian Lavery,
National Maritime Museum, Greenwich

Pedro de Medina
L'art de naviguer (1554)
Introduction by Carla Rahn Phillips,
University of Minnesota

Thomas Pownall
The administration of the colonies (4th ed., 1768)
Introduction by Daniel A. Baugh, Cornell University,
and Alison Gilbert Olson,
University of Maryland, College Park

*St. Barthélemy and the Swedish West India Company:
A selection of printed documents, 1784-1821*
Introduction by John B. Hattendorf,
Naval War College

John Seller
Practical navigation (1680)
Introduction by Michael Richey,
Royal Institute of Navigation

*Shipbuilding Timber for the British Navy:
Parliamentary papers, 1729-1792*
Introduction by R. J. B. Knight,
National Maritime Museum, Greenwich

Jean Taisnier
A very necessarie and profitable booke concerning navigation (1585?)
Introduction by Uwe Schnall,
Deutsches Schiffahrtsmuseum, Bremerhaven

Lodovico de Varthema
Die ritterlich un[d] lobwirdig Rayss (1515)
Introduction by George Winius,
University of Leiden

Gerrit de Veer
The true and perfect description of three voyages (1609)
Introduction by Stuart M. Frank,
Kendall Whaling Museum

Isaak Vossius
A treatise concerning the motion of the seas and winds (1677)
together with
De motu marium et ventorum (1663)
Introduction by Margaret Deacon,
University of Southampton

Marine Architecture

Directions for Carrying on a Ship

(1739)

A Facsimile Reproduction
With an Introduction by

BRIAN LAVERY

Published for the
JOHN CARTER BROWN LIBRARY
by
SCHOLARS' FACSIMILES & REPRINTS
DELMAR, NEW YORK
1993

SCHOLARS' FACSIMILES & REPRINTS
ISSN 0161-7729
SERIES ESTABLISHED 1936
VOLUME 481

New matter in this edition
© 1993 Academic Resources Corporation
All rights reserved

Printed and made in the United States of America

The publication of this work was assisted by a grant from the
National Endowment for the Humanities,
an agency of the Federal government

Reproduced from a copy in,
and with the permission of,
the John Carter Brown Library
at Brown University

The text of this work is printed here actual size
with the exception of the two plates at the end
of the volume which have been greatly reduced.

Library of Congress Cataloging-in-Publication Data

Marine architecture :
directions for carrying on a ship (1739) /
a facsimile reproduction with an introduction by
Brian Lavery.
    p.   cm. —
(Scholars' Facsimiles & Reprints, ISSN 0161-7729 ; v. 481)
(Maritime History Series)
Originally published:
London : Printed for William Mount and Thomas Page, 1739.
Includes bibliographical references.
ISBN 0-8201-1481-2
1. Naval architecture—Early works to 1800.
I. John Carter Brown Library.
II. Series: Maritime history series (Delmar, N.Y.)
VM156.M294   1993
623.8'1—dc20   93-13766
CIP

Introduction

The 1739 edition of *Directions for Carrying on a Ship* (to use its shorter title) appeared at a lean time both for British naval architecture, and for books about the subject. The Royal Navy was still bound by the system of Establishments (first introduced in 1706, and revised periodically until 1745), which laid down the dimensions of each part of every type of major warship; while the merchant marine produced no new ideas of any note. The last substantial work on naval architecture had been produced by William Sutherland more than 20 years earlier, and the next would be produced by Mungo Murray in 1765.

Change was not far around the corner, however. The French Navy had already begun a shipbuilding programme that would influence the composition of the other European fleets. In 1744, George Anson was appointed to the Board of Admiralty, to begin his long task of reforming all aspects of the Royal Navy, including its ship design. William Blanckley published a good nautical dictionary in 1750, and many notable writings followed in the next decades, such as those by William Falconer, Marmaduke Stalkaart, and David Steel.

But *Marine Architecture: Directions for Carrying on a Ship* did not look forward to this—on the contrary, it looked back at least three quarters of a century, to 1664. In fact, it was almost entirely copied from three works of an earlier period—Edmund Bushnell's *Compleat Ship-Wright* of 1664, Henry Bond's *The Boate Swaine's Art or the Compleat Boat Swaine* of 1642, and Thomas Miller's *The Compleat Modellist* of 1664. No acknowledgment was given to any of the original authors. It is not likely that any of the original authors were involved in the compilation. The work first appeared in its 1739 form in 1716, by which time all three men would have been of advanced age, had they survived.

INTRODUCTION

Edmund Bushnell

Little is known about the life of Edmund Bushnell, but his *Compleat Ship-Wright* apparently sold well. It had reached its third edition by 1669, and its sixth by the end of the century. It had originally been published by George Hurlock in London, but several editions were published by Fisher, Passenger, Boulter and Smith. By the sixth edition of 1669, it had been taken over by Richard Mount, and in 1716 it apparently appeared in two separate editions, both by Richard Mount. One carried the original title, while the other originated the "Directions for Carrying on a Ship" title. This edition was the first to use passages from Bond and Miller to cover the subjects of masts and rigging. This was reprinted by Mount and Page in 1736, again in 1739, and finally in 1748.

In fact, the firm of Mount and Page was a direct descendant of that run by George Hurlock. Due to mergers of one kind or another, the same organization changed its name. A key event occurred in 1682, when an apprentice named Richard Mount married Sarah Fisher, the daughter of his master William Fisher, and was taken into the business. Thomas Page, a relative by marriage, entered the business around 1700, and the firm became known as Mount and Page.

Bushnell's aims

Interestingly enough, the Mount and Page editions of Bushnell omitted the original introduction, which was very revealing about the status of the working shipwright. Bushnell was critical of the "long experienced shipwrights," because of their failure to pass on the skills of the naval architect to the majority of their apprentices.

> Yet their knowledge they desire to keep to themselves, or at least among so small a number as they can; for though some have many servants [i.e., apprentices], and by indenture (I suppose) bound to teach them all alike the same art and mystery that he himself useth; yet it may be he may teach some one, and the rest must be kept

INTRODUCTION

ignorant, so that those shipwrights, although bred by such knowing men, yet they are able to teach their servants nothing, more than to hew, or dub, to fay a piece when it is moulded to his place assigned, or the like.[1]

This is possibly the first evidence of a split that was to become much more evident in future years, between the manual work of the shipwright and the theoretical skills of the naval architect. It was certainly reflected in the royal dockyards of the eighteenth century, where some boys were apprenticed to the master shipwright of the yard, and could expect to rise to the higher ranks, while the majority were apprenticed to ordinary workmen and were not likely to rise above that station themselves. Despite this, naval architecture was not recognized as a separate profession in England until the nineteenth century.

The Combined Volume

Bushnell's reason for including these observations in his 1664 book is significant and particularly appropriate to the present context. He considered it likely that many of the less well educated shipwrights might find themselves "removed from England to Virginia or New England, or the like countries, where timber is plenty for their use." But such shipwrights "through their ignorance,"[2] would not be able to undertake ship design. His work was intended to fill this gap, and in that sense, if successful, might have contributed to the early development of American shipbuilding.

The preface to *Directions for Carrying on a Ship* goes some way to explain the publisher's intended market for the combined Bushnell-Miller-Bond volume. The main purpose of the volume, the preface claims, is to collect information on building, masting, and rigging in a way that had not been made available to the public before. It was aimed mainly at "the young mariner," who would perhaps not be so immediately critical of its defects; though it was also intended for ship's carpenters and boatswains. It seems to have been an attempt to

INTRODUCTION

open up a new market among young shipwrights after the original one had begun to close following the publication of William Sutherland's much superior work The Shipbuilder's Assistant, by Mount, Bell and Smith, in 1711.

Bushnell's Writing

Directions for Carrying on a Ship, like Bushnell's Compleat Shipwright, begins with simple geometrical propositions, and is quite illuminating about the methods used to draw parallels, right angles and scales. It then launches into explaining the method of drawing the draught of the ship. Essentially there are three separate plans: the side view or sheer draught; the midship section, or cross-section at the widest part of the ship; and a rather schematic view from above which is essential for producing the three-dimensional shape of the ship. This is drawn just below the sheer draught, almost as part of it, and can be found among the plates at the end of the book; the midship section is to be found on page 12.

Bushnell's writing is concise. The whole system of ship design is described in ten pages.[3] He relies heavily on rules of proportion established empirically over the years and handed from generation to generation. For example, "The rack [rake] of the stem is now allow'd to be three fourths of the breadth of the ship."[4] Most of the proportions are based on the breadth in this way, and the dimension of the breadth itself has already been established in the first lines of the same page, as a third of the length of the keel. He goes on to describe the drawing of the stem and stern posts—the former an arc of a circle, and the latter a straight line. He places the intended waterline, although he offers no guarantee that the ship will actually float at that level. Externally, he adds the thicker pieces of plank known as wales, and internally, he draws out the decks. He is not very helpful when he states that "For the heights between decks and steerage, cabin and fore-castle, those heights are commonly mentioned in the contract by the master or owners building."[5]

INTRODUCTION

The Midship Section

Next he turns to the midship section, which consists of four main parts, two straight lines, and two arcs of circles, on each side. Compared with what evolved later, this is a very simple section. Even Deane in 1670 had three arcs below the broadest part of the section: two above, with a single straight line. Eighteenth-century draughtsmen commonly added at least one more straight line.

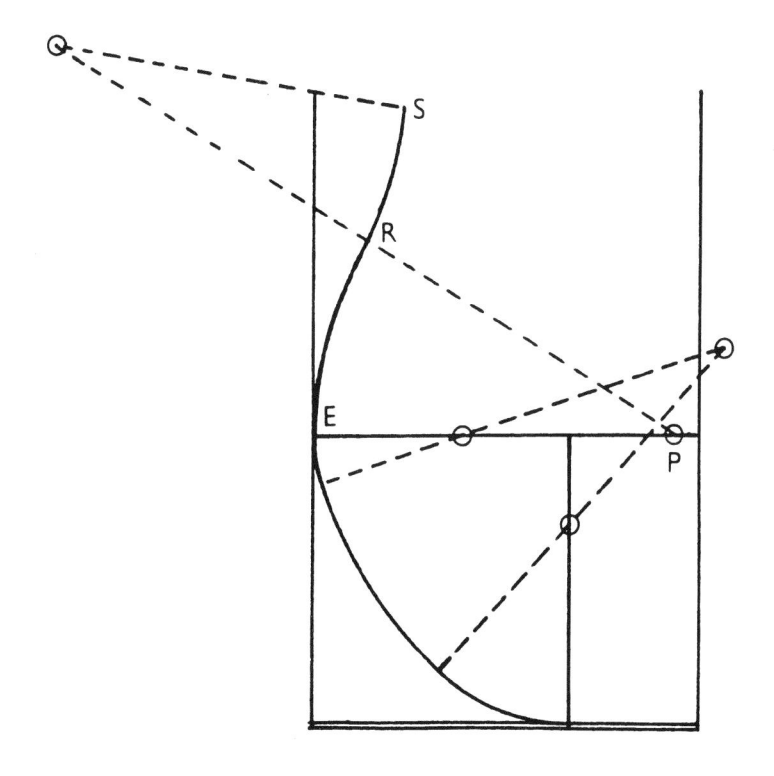

A midship section as drawn by Anthony Deane in 1670

INTRODUCTION

The midship section is drawn within a rectangle, with a vertical center line drawn in. The flat, or almost flat, part at the center and bottom of the ship was known as the floor. Bushnell recommends a broad one, giving the stability and greater carrying capacity required of a merchantman. The rest of the hull below the main breadth is formed by two "sweeps" or arcs of circle. The method of calculating the diameters and positions of the centers of these, using diagonals divided into ninths, is unusual and it has not survived in any other treatise on naval architecture. The first sweep, generally known as the floor sweep, is of small diameter. It meets the end of the floor as a tangent, and has its center directly above that point. The second sweep, known as the reconciling sweep on more conventional designs, forms a tangent with the floor sweep. It has its center on the level of the maximum breadth, and it has a relatively large diameter so that its center is on the opposite side of the center line. It continues above the maximum breadth, and forms a tangent with the straight line which continues the shape of the section up to the top of the side. This allows for considerable narrowing of the hull above the maximum breadth, known as the "tumble-home."

The Shape of the Hull

The next stage is to draw the four lines which will give the rest of the shape of the hull. In the sheer plan, Bushnell has drawn the two "rising lines" or "hanging lines," and in the plan view below it are the equivalent "narrowing lines." Essentially these are two lines, drawn in different planes. The rising and narrowing lines of the breadth define the position of the maximum breadth through the various stations along the length of the ship, while the rising and narrowing lines of the floor perform the same function for the outer end of the floor.

The rising line of the floor is formed by two circles and a straight line. The latter is parallel to, and slightly above the keel at midships. The two circles are tangential to that line, and meet the stempost and sternpost respectively, at the height of the waterline.

INTRODUCTION

This was enough to define their diameters for the builder. The rising line of floor was regarded as a very important feature of the underwater hull of a ship, and the subject of much passionate debate among shipwrights. Bushnell and Deane both used circles to form it, but others used ellipses or more complex mathematical formulae. The rising line of the breadth, on the other hand, was simpler and was generally formed by a single curve.

To draw the narrowing line of the breadth, the draughtsman starts with the given breadth of 20 feet, and plots this under the sheer draught. To narrow this at the bows, he draws an arc of a circle, tangential to the straight line representing the breadth, and meeting it at the same distance from the bows as where the stempost begins to rise. Aft, he has to draw the transom, and this is worked out by a proportion of the breadth. To meet the outer end of the transom, he draws another circle tangential to the line parallel to the keel.

The narrowing line of the floor was formed in a roughly similar way. A line was drawn parallel to the keel, four feet away to represent half the floor breadth of eight feet. This is similarly tapered towards the ends of the ship, although the text is rather vague about the method—it merely mentions a "crooked line." It was presumably intended to be an arc of a circle like the others, unless Bushnell believed that he had discovered some new method, and intended to keep it secret.

Vertical lines are drawn on the sheer draught, to represent the stations of the frames which will form the final shape of the hull; conventionally, they are drawn up only as far as the height of the rising line of floor at that station, but they are also represented on the plan view. Those in midships are numbered with and those aft with a circle, those forward with letters, and those aft with numbers.

Finally in this section, Bushnell indicates the need for the toptimber line, "signifying the breadth of the vessel at the top of the side."[6] Apart from telling us that the ship is 10 feet wide at this point at the top of the poop, he is rather vague about how it is to be drawn.

INTRODUCTION

The Use of the Mould Loft Floor

To complete the shape of the hull, it is necessary to draw out the shape of each frame. Unusually, Bushnell does not do this on paper, but draws it full size on the mould loft floor—"some house that has some room or other place broad enough to demonstrate the breadth of the vessel, and height enough for the top of the poop in the length of the room."[7] The first stage is to draw a rectangle with a center line, inside which the frames will be drawn. This is a full-size version of the rectangle used for the midship section, but it extends upwards because the ship is higher at the bows and stern than in midships. Also drawn on the floor is a horizontal line at the height of maximum breadth in midships,[8] and verticals at the positions of the lower ends of the floor sweep.[9] This forms a grid within which the other frames can be drawn.

The positions of the sweeps for each individual frame can be found on the sheer draught, by means of the narrowing and rising lines. Bushnell gives examples of this for frames 3, 6, and 13. These are all drawn on the left hand side of the grid, because the right hand side was to be used for frames forward of midships. Having thus found the positions of the maximum breadth and the end of the floor sweep, it is easy to position the centres of the sweeps. Apparently these retain the same diameter throughout the length of the ship.

Bushnell and Deane

Bushnell's method was old-fashioned even in 1664, and Deane's Doctrine of 1670 shows two distinct advances. He draws the frames on paper first, making it much easier to construct waterlines, or horizontal sections, on the draught. These help to check that the lines are fair, without the local irregularities that can be created by the standard method. Secondly, Deane varies the diameter of the circles, especially the sweep at the height of the breadth. He tends to reduce its diameter towards the bow and stern, and this allows a much greater flexibility in creating the shape of the hull. He does not explain how

INTRODUCTION

he decides the diameters of these circles, but perhaps it is related to the use of waterlines for fairing. Bushnell's method might have served for small merchant ships, and perhaps it was better adapted to the skills and facilities of a small shipyard, but it would not have been effective for the increasingly large warships which Deane built.

Ship Construction

So far, Bushnell has described only the outside edge of each frame. The frame tends to taper or "diminish" from bottom to top, so he provides a scale, shown on the right-hand side of page 16, to show how this is measured. In the case of frames towards the bow and stern, where the rising line of floor has risen above the keel, some method is needed to link the frame with the keel. His instructions for doing this are a little obscure, but it seems that a template forming the arc of a circle was made, placed so that it passed through the corner of the keel and formed a tangent with the floor sweep, and a line was drawn out. This formed the lower shape of the hull in these areas.

Bushnell also describes methods of making "sir marks" on the moulds, so that these can be transferred to the timbers, thus ensuring that the whole assembly will come together accurately; but this is as close as he gets to the actual building of the ship. In this respect, the title "carrying on a ship, from the first laying of her keel to her actual going to sea," is quite misleading.

Arithmetic and Rigging

The rest of the section taken from Bushnell's treatise deals with arithmetic, and it is less interesting in the present context. However, the method of calculating the size of a circle needed to enclose certain points must have been quite useful to shipwrights, and the pages of square roots, etc., were necessary for his original intended audidnce, who expected to find themselves in remote parts of the world without any other sources of reference. He also provides some

INTRODUCTION

information on the measuring of ships, but this is slightly more advanced than might be expected. The official formulae (keel × breadth × half breadth divided by 100 or 94) gives no real indication of the real displacement of a ship, because, as Bushnell was aware, it did not take account of "the fullness or sharpness of those vessels."[10] He allows for the possibility of actually calculating the displacement of the ship by measuring each individual part. Samuel Pepys gives Deane the credit for inventing a method for doing this, but even a rather backward shipwright like Bushnell was aware of the possibilities in 1664.

Bushnell's 1664 work on rigging is repeated in Chapter XII of *Directions for Carrying on a Ship*, which deals with masts and spars. Again rules of proportion play a very important part, and nothing is said about the construction of the spars themselves. Bushnell's final chapter, "Concerning rowing of ships, when they are becalmed," is omitted from *Directions for Carrying on a Ship*. This dealt with a system of oars linked to the ship's capstan.

Henry Bond

From page 53 onwards, the book is a blend of works of Henry Bond and Thomas Miller. Bond was a "teacher of navigation, surveying and other parts of the mathematics." He published the first edition of *The Boate Swaines Art* in 1642, and by 1676 he had added an extra section entitled "A Plaine and Easie Rule to Rigg any Ship by the length of her masts and yards, without any further trouble." The whole of this section, including the title, was incorporated in *Directions*.[11] Parts of *The Boat Swainers Art* are also used.[12] By the 1670 edition, Bond was being published by Fisher and Hurlock, and so the work came into the possession of Mount and Page in the same way as with Bushnell.

INTRODUCTION

Thomas Miller

Miller's *Compleat Modellist* first appeared in 1642, and by 1684 was being published by Hurlock, another part of the succession leading to Mount and Page. In *Directions*, the tables entitled "Of rigging a ship"[13] were taken from this, although the linking passage[14] appears to be original. Also taken from Miller were the four plates A, B, C, and D at the end, and the description of them on page 77. The origin of the tables on cordage and weight of cables[15] has not been traced, nor has that describing "The method used in Deptford Yard."[16] Apart from that, only a few short linking passages[17] are original to *Directions for Carrying on a Ship*.

The mixture of Bushnell, Bond, and Miller, not surprisingly, is often confused and contradictory, and was certainly out of date by 1739. The spritsails used in the diagrams and tables, fitted to a spritsail topmast extending vertically from the end of the bowsprit, were obsolete by 1720, even on the largest ships. On the other hand new ropes, such as bobstays, had been introduced around 1680, and there is no mention of these, although they were widely used.

Progress in naval architecture was slow in the early eighteenth century, but not so slow that Bushnell's work was still valid after 75 years. Even on its publication in 1664, it had been rather dated in its method of drawing the sections of the hull, and it was completely obsolete by 1739. However, we tend to judge progress in naval architecture by what happened in the more advanced naval yards. The practices of the builders of small merchant ships are much more obscure to historians, and *Directions for Carrying on a Ship* gives us some clues here. Its survival in print, in one form or another, over more than three quarters of a century tells us something about the state of the nautical book market. It must have sold to successive generations of midshipmen and shipwrights, though it is doubtful if it had any real relevance to practical shipbuilding in Britain after about 1715.

BRIAN LAVERY
National Maritime Museum, Greenwich

INTRODUCTION

NOTES

1. *The Compleat Shipwright*, "To the Reader" (pages unnumbered).
2. *The Compleat Shipwright*, "To the Reader."
3. *Directions*, pp. 9-19. Unless otherwise stated, the following page numbers refer to the facsimile published here.
4. Ibid., p. 9.
5. Ibid., p. 11.
6. Ibid., p. 15.
7. Idem.
8. Marked "IK" on p. 16.
9. FE and GH
10. Ibid., p. 46.
11. Ibid., pp. 56-58.
12. Ibid., pp. 53, beginning "The first, which is the most rational way," is extracted from a much longer passage. "A table of the lengths and thickness of the masts and yards" is reproduced in full (pp. 53-55), as is "A Table of the names, the sizes . . ." Ibid., pp. 60-66).
13. Ibid., pp. 68-76.
14. Ibid., p. 67.
15. Ibid., pp. 79, 80.
16. Ibid., p. 55.
17. Ibid., p. 56, "Having given directions . . . "; p. 67, "A table of the thickness . . . ,"; p. 77, paragraph beginning "Having made a scale . . . ."

INTRODUCTION

SUGGESTIONS FOR FURTHER READING

Contemporary works on naval architecture:

Anonymous. *A Treatise on Shipbuilding and a Treatise on Rigging Written About 1620-1625*, ed. W. Salisbury and R. C. Anderson (London: Society for Nautical Research Occasional Publications no. 6, 1958).

Bushnell, Edmund. *The Compleat Shipwright* (1st ed., London, 1664).

Deane, Sir Anthony. *Deane's Doctrine of Naval Architecture, 1670*, ed. Brian Lavery (London: Conway Maritime Press, 1981).

Murray, Mungo. *A Treatise on Shipbuilding and Navigation* (London, 1765).

Sutherland, William. *Britain's Glory, or Shipbuilding Unvail'd* (London, 1717).

—————. *The Shipbuilder's Assistant* (London, 1711; rpt. Rotherfield: Jean Boudriot Publications, 1990).

Modern Works:

Adams, Thomas R. *The Non-Cartographical Works Published by Mount and Page* (London: Bibliographical Society, 1985).

Anderson, R. C. "Eighteenth-Century Books on Shipbuilding and Rigging," *Mariners Mirror*, vol X, (1924), pp. 53-64.

Chaplin, W. R. "A Seventeenth Century Chart Publisher," in *American Neptune*, vol. VIII (1948), pp. 302-24.

Lavery, B. *The Ship of the Line, Vol II, Construction and Fittings* (London; Conway Maritime Press, 1984).

INTRODUCTION

White, David. "Understanding Ships Draughts," in *Model Shipwright*, vols. 46, 48, 50, 52, 54, 56 (1983-85).

I am grateful to David H. Roberts, Lars Bruzelius, John Hattendorf, and Tom Adams for help with the bibliography of Bushnell.

MARINE ARCHITECTURE:
OR
DIRECTIONS
FOR
Carrying on a SHIP, from the firſt Laying of the Keel to her actual Going to SEA.

SHEWING,

I. The Proportions uſed by Experienced SHIP-WRIGHTS in Building, both *Geometrically* and *Arithmetically* performed. Alſo the Making, Marking, and Ordering a Bend of Moulds: With a large Table of the SQUARE ROOT, and Directions concerning the Meaſuring of SHIPS.

II. Directions for MASTING and YARDING of any Ship, or making both in a juſt Proportion to the Ship, and to one another; both as to Length and Thickneſs. Alſo Directions for Cutting out the Sails.

III. The Boatſwain's Art, Shewing how to RIGG a SHIP, or to know the Length and Thickneſs of every Rope exactly; with CORDAGE TABLES, to know by Inſpection the Weight of any Rope, whoſe Length and Thickneſs is given; and the Conſtructing or Making of the ſaid Tables.

The whole Illuſtrated with SCHEMES and DRAUGHTS to make it intelligible to all Capacities.

LONDON: Printed for *William Mount* and *Thomas Page*, at the Poſtern on *Tower-Hill*. 1739.

PREFACE.

THE useful Subject of Building and Rigging of Ships, having been scatteringly handled in different Books or Pamphlets, according to the different Branches thereof; some upon Building, others upon Rigging, &c. we have, for the Instruction of Persons in those Faculties, collected what is most useful in Building, Masting, Yarding, and Rigging of Ships, under the general Title of Marine Architecture, not doubting but it will answer the Purpose of Ship-Carpenters, Boatswains, &c. as well as the Young Mariner; for all whose Use it is intended.

THE

THE CONTENTS.

Chap. I. *Of Geometrical Problems* — Page 5
Chap. II. *Of the Scale* — — — Pag. 7
Chap. III. *Concerning the Drawing your Draught upon Paper* Pag. 9
Chap. IV. *Shewing how to sweep out a Bend of Moulds upon a Flat for a Ship of twenty Foot broad* — — Pag. 11
Chap. V. *The Description of the Rising Lines aftward on, and forward on; with the Narrowing Lines, and Lines of Breadth: As also the Narrowing of Lines at the Top of the Timbers* — Pag. 13
Chap. VI. *The Making and Graduating, or Marking a Bend of Moulds* Pag. 15
Chap. VII. *Arithmetically shewing how to frame the Body of a Ship by Segments of Circles, being the true way to examine the truth of a Bow, with a Table of the Square Root ready extracted* Pag. 20
Chap. VIII. *How to extract the Square Root, and compose the foregoing Table of Squares.* — Pag. 34
Chap. IX. *The Description and Use of the Table of Squares* Pag. 39
Chap. X. *Shewing how to hang a Rising Line by several Sweeps, to make it rounder aftward, than at the Beginning of the same* Pag. 41
Chap. XI. *Concerning the Measuring of Ships* — Pag. 45
Chap. XII. *Rules for Masting and Yarding Ships in Proportion to their Dimensions; and first, To find the Length of the Main-mast, which in a great measure governs all the rest; the Length by the Keel, the Breadth at the Beam, and the Depth in the Hold being known* — Pag. 50
Chap. XIII. *Of Rigging a Ship, first for the Length of each Rope* Pag. 56
And then for their Thickness — — Pag. 67
Chap. XIV. *The Use of the Cuts A, B, C and D at the End of the Book.* Pag. 77

THE

THE
Compleat SHIP-WRIGHT.

CHAP. I.
Of Geometrical PROBLEMS.

BEfore we proceed to draw the Draught of any Ship or Veſſel, it will be neceſſary to be acquainted with ſome Terms in *Geometry*: As, To know what a Point and a Line meaneth, which every Book treating of *Geometry* plainly teacheth, and therefore we ſhall paſs that by, ſuppoſing that none will endeavour to ſtudy the Art of a SHIP-WRIGHT, that is ignorant of theſe Things. And therefore, leaving theſe Definitions, I will proceed to ſome Geometrical PROBLEMS neceſſary to this Art.

PROBLEM I.
How to draw a Parallel Line

Parallel Lines are ſuch as are equidiſtant one from another in all Parts, and are thus drawn: Draw a Line of what Length you pleaſe (according to your Occaſion) as the Line *A B*, then open the Compaſſes to what diſtance you pleaſe, or as your Occaſions require, and ſet one Foot of the Compaſſes towards one End of the given Line, as at *A*, with the other Foot make a Piece of an Arch of a Circle, over or under the given Line, as the Arch *C*; keeping the Compaſſes then at the ſame Diſtance, make ſuch another Arch towards the other End of the Line, ſetting

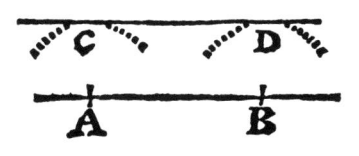

one

one Foot in *B*, and with the other defcribe the Arch *D*, then laying a Ruler to he outfide of thefe two Arches, fo that it may exactly touch them, draw the Line *C D*, which will be parallel to the given Line *A B*, or equidiftant; for fo fignifieth the Word *Parallel*, to be of equal diftance.

PROB. II.

How to erect a Perpendicular, from a Point in a right Line given.

Let there be a Point given in the Line *A B*, as the Point *C*, whereon to raife a Perpendicular.

Set one Foot of the Compaffes in the given Point *C*, and open them to what Diftance you pleafe, as to the Point *E*; make a little Mark at *E*, and keeping the Compaffes at the fame diftance, turn them about, and make a Mark at the Point *F*, in the Line *A B*: Then remove the Compaffes to one of thofe Marks at *E*, or *F*, and fetting one Foot faft therein, as at the Point *F*, open the other Foot wider, and therewith draw a fmall Arch over the Point *C*; as the Arch *D*: then keeping the Compaffes at the fame diftance, remove them to *E*, and fetting one Foot in *E*, with the other Foot draw another little Arch, fo as to crofs the former Arch in the Point *D*; through the croffing of thefe two Arches *A D*, draw a Line to the given Point *C*, as the Line *D C* which fhall be perpendicular to the Line *A B*.

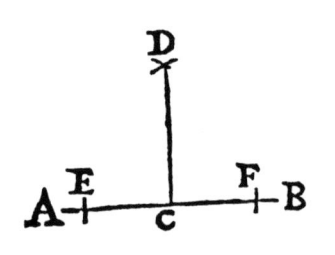

PROB. III.

To raife a Perpendicular at the End of a Line.

Draw a Line at pleafure, or according to your Work, as the Line *A B*; on the End thereof as at *B*, fet one Foot of the Compaffes, and open them to what widenefs you pleafe as to *C*; then
keeping

keeping one Foot of the Compasses in *C*, and at the same Distance, remove the Foot that was in *B*, to the Point *D*, in the Line *A B*: Then (keeping the Compasses still at the same Distance) lay a Ruler to the Points *D* and *C*, and with your Compasses set off the Distance from *C* to *E*: Lastly, draw the Line *E B*, which will be perpendicular or square to the End of the given Line *A B*.

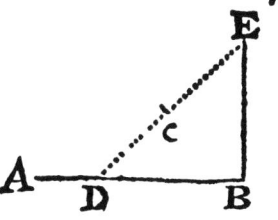

PROB. IV.

From a Point given, to let fall a Perpendicular upon a Line given.

From the Point *C*, let it be required to let fall a Perpendicular upon the Line *A B*. Proceed thus: Fix one Foot of the Compasses in the Point *C*, and open them to a greater distance than just to the Line *A B*, and make with the same extent the two Marks *E* and *F*, in the given Line *A B*, then divide the Distance between the two Points *E* and *F*, into two equal Parts in the Point *D*; then lay a Ruler to the given Point *C*, and to the Point *D*, and draw the Line *C D*, which will be Perpendicular to the given Line *A B*.

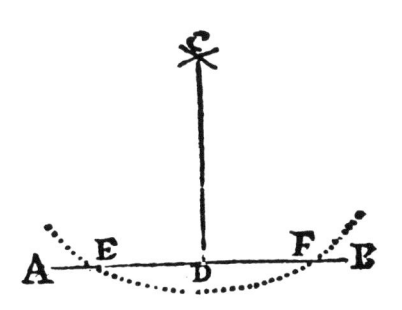

CHAP. II.
Of your SCALE.

BEing perfect in the raising and letting fall of Perpendiculars, and in the drawing of Parallel Lines, you may proceed to Draught: But first I will unfold to you the Use of a Diagonal Scale of Inches

and

and Feet, whoſe Uſe is to repreſent a Foot Meaſure, or a Rule ſo ſmall, that a Ship of 100 Foot by the Keel, may be demonſtrated on a common Sheet of Paper to be ſo many Foot long, and ſo many Foot broad, of ſuch a depth, and of ſuch a height between the Decks. And therein, the firſt thing to be conſidered is the Length of the Platform, and of the Veſſel you intend to demonſtrate, to the End you may make your Scale as large as you can; becauſe the larger your Scale is, the larger will your Draught be, and ſo the Meaſure of the Demonſtration will be the larger, and more eaſy to unfold. The Scale adjoining conſiſteth (as you ſee) of 12 Feet in all, 11 thereof are marked with Figures downwards, beginning at 1, 2, 3, 4, and ſo to 11: The firſt at the Top is ſubdivided into Inches by Diagonal Lines, as the Diſtance between the firſt Line of the Scale, and the firſt Diagonal Line is one Inch, the ſecond is two, and the third three Inches, and ſo to ſix. The way to demonſtrate the Scale, you ſee, is very eaſy: Draw ſeven Lines parallel to each other, and of what Length you pleaſe, to retain what Number of Feet you pleaſe; then begin at the Top, ſet off with the Compaſſes the Length of your Feet both alow and aloft; then draw Lines thwart the Parallel Lines to every Foot of the Scale, and ſet Numbers to them, (beginning at the ſecond Foot 1, and to the third 2, to the fourth 3, and ſo forward, leaving the firſt Foot to be divided into Inches by the Diagonal Lines; as you ſee in the Scale annex'd.

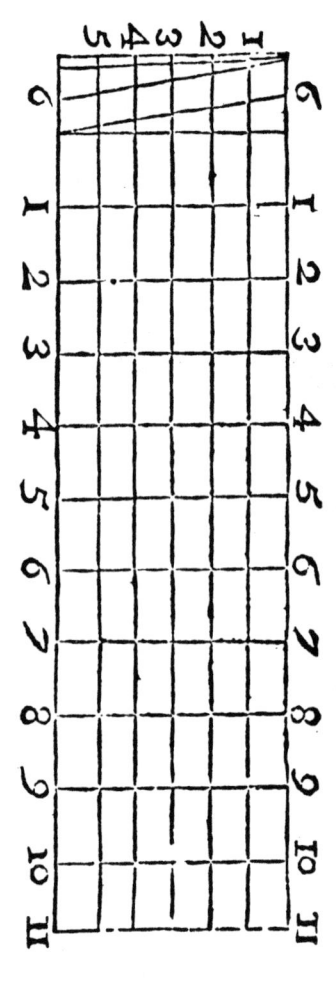

CHAP.

CHAP. III.

Concerning the drawing your Draught upon Paper.

HAving fitted your Scale ready, draw a Line to represent the Keel of the Ship, as you see in the Draught following of 60 Foot long by the Keel, and 20 Foot broad: The strait Line representeth the Keel, and is marked with *A B*. Then draw a Line underneath of equal length, to represent the bottom of the Keel. Then next you may proceed to the Stern-post, as the Line *A C* will signify the foreside or the inside thereof, racking the one quarter of his length aft, and for the length of the Stern-post it must be directed to the Built of the Ship, as whether she be to be a deep Ship or a shallow Ship, so that the draught of the Water ought to be respected first, and then the lying of the Ports for the convenience of Ordinance, for that the upper Transome of the Buttock, commonly is just under the Gun-room Ports, to the upper edge of the said Transome, we understand the length of the Stern-post, altho' if the Stern-post were continued to the height of the Tiller, and another Transome fay'd there for the Tiller to run on, it would steddy the quarters of the Vessel very much, and do good service.

The rack of the Stem is now allow'd to be three fourths of the breadth of the Ship, which in this Ship of twenty Foot broad, is fifteen Foot, which is enough, for too much rack with the Stem doth a great deal of damage to any Ship, if we consider that in this small Vessel, had we given 5 Foot more rack, all the weight of the Ship's Head and Bolt-sprit, Fore-mast, Manger, Halses, Brest-hooks aloft, had been so much farther forward, where there would have been want of Body, to support it, so that it must of necessity be a detriment to the Vessel when she saileth against a Head-Sea, and a great strain to her. Now it will be very good to spend as much of this rack as we can under the Water, for it will help the Ship to keep a good Wind, by giving her something more Body in the Water.

Next draw the Water-line, in the following Draught signified by the Line *D P*; it is drawn to 9 Foot height afore, and to 10 Foot height abaft from the upper edge of the Keel, and higher abaft than

than afore, for the moſt Ships ſail by the Stern, and alſo for that the Guns ſhould lie ſomething higher abaft than afore from the Water.

Then proceed to hanging of the Waals, and here you ſee the lower Waal drawn from the Head of the Stern-poſt, to ſignify that it ſhould lie againſt the end of the Tranſome, that the Tranſome Knees might be bolted to the Waals without board to one Foot and an half under the Water-line, a little below the middle of the Water-line, and at 9 Foot high on the Stem, and the next Waal parallel to the lower Waal, one Foot and an half aſunder, ſo that the upper Waal will lie juſt at the Water's edge, in the Mid-ſhips; the upper edge of the Gun-deck will lie one Foot above the Water-line abaft, and a half Foot above Water on the Stem; ſo then letting the lower Sell of the Ports be two Foot from the Gun-decks, the lower edge of the Ports will be three Foot from the Water abaft, and two Foot and a half afore, in the middle of the Gun-deck 2 Foot 9 Inches, ſufficient for ſo ſmall a Veſſel, a greater Veſſel would require to have the Guns ſomething farther from the Water: Then if another Waal be required, firſt ſet off the Ports in their places, that the Waal may lie above the Ports, or elſe he would be cut with the Ports in pieces, the upper Deck with height reſpecting the bigneſs of the Ship, having reſpect to not over building ſmall Ships to damage their bearing of Sail.

Then for the Head, the length of the Knee would be two thirds of the breadth, ſo then the Knee of the Head in this Draught will be 12 Foot 8 Inches long, and for this place, as low as conveniently he can, provided that the Rails of the Head come not foul of the Hals-holes, becauſe that in placing of the Knee low, giveth room to round the Head, and ſteeve it to content. The place of the Knee will be at, or very near, the upper Waal, the upper edge of the Knee againſt the upper edge of the upper Harping, which will be very well for the lower Cheeks of the Head to be fayed againſt; for by that means they will be clear of any Seam to avoid Leakings, and will very well bolt the end of the Harping, if a Breſt-hook be faſtned alſo within board againſt them, it will very well faſten all together.

Then for the ſteeving of him, and rounding the Knee, a regard muſt be had to the lying of the Bolt-ſprit, leaving room enough for the Lion and Scrowl under the Bolt-ſprit. Then for the rounding of the Rails, round them moſt at the after ends.

For

for the heights between Decks and Steerage, Cabin and Fore-castle, those heights are commonly mentioned in Contract by the Master or Owners building.

CHAP. IV.

How to sweep out the Bend of Moulds upon a Flat, for a Ship of twenty Foot broad. See the following Figure.

First draw a Line, as the Line AB, then in the middle thereof, as at the Point C, raise a Perpendicular, as in the Line Cm, perpendicular to the Line AB; then set off the half breadth, on either side, at the Points A and B, and draw the two Lines IA and KB, parallels to CD, signifying the breadth of the Vessel 20 Foot; then draw the two Lines EF and HG, signifying the breadth of the Floor thwart Ships, 8 Foot, more than one third part of the breadth, though that was the old Proportion; and according to that it should have been but 6 Foot 8 Inches.

Herein any may do as they please, give more or less; my Judgment is, rather more than less: For that it maketh a Vessel carry more in Burden, and I conceive if it be well ended forward, it will not damage the Sailing: I also think, it doth stiffen a Vessel on this account. Our *English* Vessels have been used to have their breadth lying at the height of the half breadth, then observing ⅓ breadth for the length of the Floor thwart Ships, it maketh the Vessels Body to be very near a Circle, as is a Cask, which causeth such Vessels to be easy to flew in the Water: But the best way to make a Vessel stiff is; that the half breadth be more than the draught of Water, which causeth that the Body be stronger in the Water, and will not flew so easily. Now to sweep out the Sides under Water, draw the Diagonal Lines DA and DB, then divide the Diagonal Lines into 9 parts, and set off two of them from the Corners A and B to the point e, then set off the dead Rising, which is of 4 Inches, 1 Inch to a Foot, for half the breadth represented in the Figure, by the little Line parallel to FG: From which dead Rising, take with the Compasses the Distance that will draw a piece of an Arch from f to e, and so as one Foot of the Compasses stand in the Line EF, and exactly touch the Points at the dead Rising, at f or g, and touch also the Point e over which Point

B 2 falls

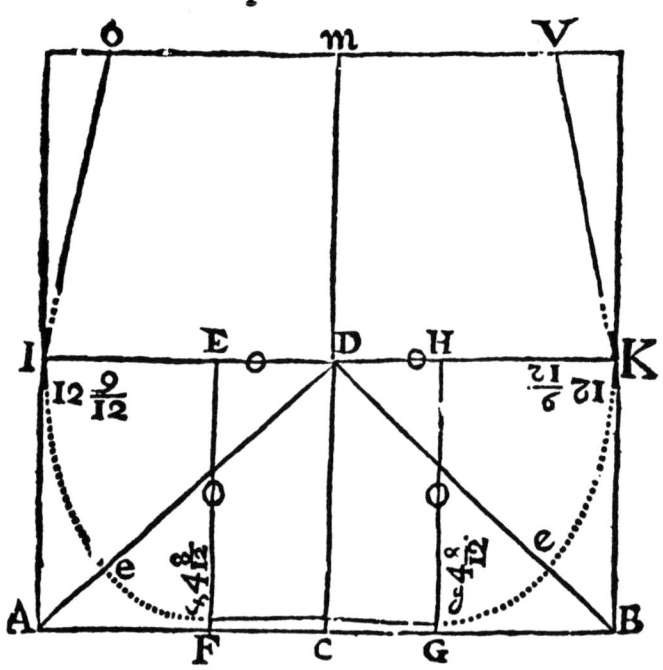

falls at ⊙, in *EF* or ⊙ in *HG*, wherewith I describe the Arch *ef*, or *eg*, which is by the Scale in the Draught 4 Foot 8 Inches: Then for the other part of the side upwards, seek for a Point in the breadth Line *IK*, at which, if one Foot of the Compasses be set, and the other Foot opened to the extreme breadth, will also draw, or signify an Arch to meet with the other lower Arch, on the Diagonal Line at *e*, which is at the Points ⊙ and ⊙; thus the Point ⊙, between *D* and *K* near *H* sweepeth the contrary side *I e*, and so the Point ⊙ between *D* and *I*, near *E*, sweepeth the contrary side *e K*; extend the same sweep also above the Breadth-line above Water 3 or 4 Foot, the length of this Sweep is 12 Foot 9 Inches: Then set off the Tumbling-home, at the height of the two first Haanses, at the Main-mast, and Fore-castle two Foot of a side; then draw a Line from the said 2 Foot of narrowing, at the Points *O* and *V*, till it break off on the back of the Sweep, on either side. And this kind of Demonstration I conceive most suitable to our following Discourse of *Arithmetical Work.*

CHAP.

CHAP. V.

The Description of the Rising-lines aftward on, and forward on ; with the Narrowing-lines, and Lines of Breadth; as also the Narrowing-lines at the top of the Timbers.

DRaw a Hanging-line on the Draught, from the middle of the Keel to the height of the Water-line, on the Post which will be the Rising-line, as the Line *D E* ; this Line *D E* is supposed to be swept, or drawn by a Semidiameter of a Circle, extended on a Perpendicular raised at the Point *E*, for if it be shorter than such a Semidiameter of the true Circle, it will make a fuller Line than it should be, and so must not be so long, or else it will make a breach at the beginning of the Line ; thus, if the Center be supposed to be abaft such a Perpendicular, that should draw a Rising-line abaft, I say, that it will shorten the Rising-line, and make it fuller than it should be ; or then if it be farther forward, it will be straighter than a Circle, and also be a breach at the beginning of the Rising-line, afore it should be a Circle, whose Semidiameter will be on the Perpendicular-line, at the beginning of any such Rising-line, on the Heel, either afore or abaft, and the like ought to be for all other crooked Lines, as the Narrowing-lines abaft, or afore, at the Narrowing of the Floor, or other Circular-lines, as hanging of Waals, and the like ; the way whereof I shall describe, to find the lengths of all such Sweeps by Arithmetick ; as also the true rising, narrowing of any Timber, according to the exact pieces of Circles, very useful for the setting of Bows, to try whether they hang to a true sweep or no : I shall demonstrate it, in the following Discourse, and in this place end what I intend to say : For Demonstration then, at $\frac{1}{4}$ of the Keel forward from the Post I draw a Rising-line forward to the height of the Water-line forward on the Stem, as you see the Line *O P* ; and the little Line, between these two Lines, parallel to the inside of the Keel, marked *E O*, is the dead Rising 4 Inches high, as in the bend of Moulds it is parallel to *FG*, the height of the breadth from the Mid-ship forward, is the lower edge of the upper Waal ; but aftward

ward on it is the Pricked-line, between the Water-line and the lower Waal, on the Poſt, which runneth forward to the edge of the Waal, and hath Figures ſet to it, to ſignify the places of the Timbers marked 1, 2, 3, 4, 5, to 15; as you ſee anſwers to the Figures on the Keel: And the Letters ſet forward on, ſignify the places of the Timbers forward, marked, *A*,*B*,*C*,*D*, &c. to *L*, in the middle of the Veſſel: The places marked with a Cypher, ſignify the Flats, which have only dead Riſing, altho' they ought to have (ſome of them) ſomething more dead Riſing than each other; and thoſe that have leaſt, to be placed in the middle of the reſt, that ſo there be no Clings in the Buldg, but that it have alſo a little hanging in it, it will ſeem fairer: Then I draw a ſtrait Line, parallel to the bottom of the Keel, as is the Line *FQ*, parallel to the Line *AB*, the Keel, and diſtant 10 Foot by the Scale, which is the half breadth of the Veſſel; for this Line ſignifieth a Line ſtretched from the middle of the Stern-poſt to the middle of the Stem, called by SHIP-WRIGHTS, a Ram-line: Parallel to this Middle-line I draw another Line ſtrait, marked *n m*, and is 4 Foot from the Middle line, to ſignify the half length of the Floor thwart ſhips, as in the bend of Moulds *EF* is diſtant from *DC*, 4 Foot: Then I draw a crooked Line abaft, within this Line *n m*, to ſignify the narrowing of the Floor, to bring or form the Veſſels way abaft, as you ſee the Line *i p* abaft; and afore it is repreſented by the Line *Q*: Then in this Draught I draw a Sweep, or a piece of a Circle from the Point *G*, the Mark of the Timber *G*, on the Keel, to *g* the half breadth on the Stem, ſignifying the ſweep of the Harping, and is ſwept by the breadth of the Veſſel 20 Foot: The piece of the pricked Circle abaft at the Stern, which is drawn by a Center on the Line *FG*, is the length of the Tranſome thwart the Stern, as is the Arch *FS*, the length whereof is 8 Foot, which doubled is 16 Foot, for the whole length; which is $\frac{4}{5}$, of the breadth 20 Foot, the length of the Sweep that ſweepeth it is the length of the Stern-poſt to the bottom of the Keel 14 Foot $\frac{2}{3}$ then the crooked Line from the end of the Tranſome, or from the Point *S*, and toucheth the Keel at the Point *P*. This Arch *SP*, is the Narrowing-line abaft at the breadth, and the crooked Pricked-line within the Keel, marked with *TR*, is a Riſing-line, to order a hollow Mould by the Timbers, which are placed at 2 Foot Timber and Room, as you may ſee by the Scale, and the Line drawn from the Poop to the Fore-caſtle, marked by the

The Compleat SHIP-WRIGHT. 15

the Letters *VW*, is a Line fignifying the breadth of the Veffel, at the top of the Side, from the top of the Poop to the Fore-caftle, the top of the Poop is in breadth 10 Foot, half the breadth at the Beam ; the Ufe of this Line is in ordering of the Moulds, to fteddy the Head of the Top-timber Mould, to find the breadth aloft.

C H A P. VI.

Shewing the Making and Graduating, or Marking of the Bend of Moulds.

REpair to fome Houfe that hath fome room or other place broad enough to demonftrate the breadth of the Veffel, and height enough for the top of the Poop in the length of the Room ; or elfe if you cannot find fuch a Room convenient, lay Boards together ; or Planks, that may be large enough for your Bufinefs, as in the following Scheme you fee : Firft a long Square made for the breadth of the Veffel, as in the following Figure *IABK*: Then make the Moulds by their Sweeps, and make Sir-marks to them for laying them together in their true places, firft the Mould, for the Floor being made, you may make a Sir-mark by the Line *EF*, on the head of the Floor-mould, and another on the foot of the naval Timber-mould, at the fame place, to fignify that thofe two Marks when put together, they are in their true places, and will compare fo when any Timber are moulded by them : Thofe Sir-marks muft alfo be marked off on the Timbers, and fo in putting the Timbers up in the Frame, a regard being had to compare Sir-marks with Sir-marks, each Timber will find its own place, and come to his own breadth, and give the Veffel that Form affigned her by your Draught, if it be wrought by it, and for all the other Moulds.

In making your Moulds, that they may be fmaller and fmaller upwards, and not all of a bignefs, you may meafure the depth of the fide in the Mid-fhips Circular, as it goeth from the Keel to the top of the fide, as here the fide, as it roundeth, is 26 Foot, and in depth at the Round-heads, or at the end of the Floor, is one Foot, as *mm*; and at the other end, at the head of the Timber is but half a Foot, as at *nn*, fo

then

16 *The Compleat* SHIP-WRIGHT.

then drawing two Lines, as the Lines *nm*, reprefents the diminifhing of the Moulds in thicknefs upwards, as thofe two Lines reprefenteth; as if you would find the thicknefs of the Timbers at the breadth, take your 2 Foot-rule, and meafure the length from the end of the Floor at the Point *F* and *I*, at the breadth in the crooked Body, and it is 11 Foot 9 Inches, fignified at the Sir-marks there, thofe two Lines fhew the thicknefs to be 9 Inches, and fo thick ought the Moulds to be at the breadth of the Veffel.

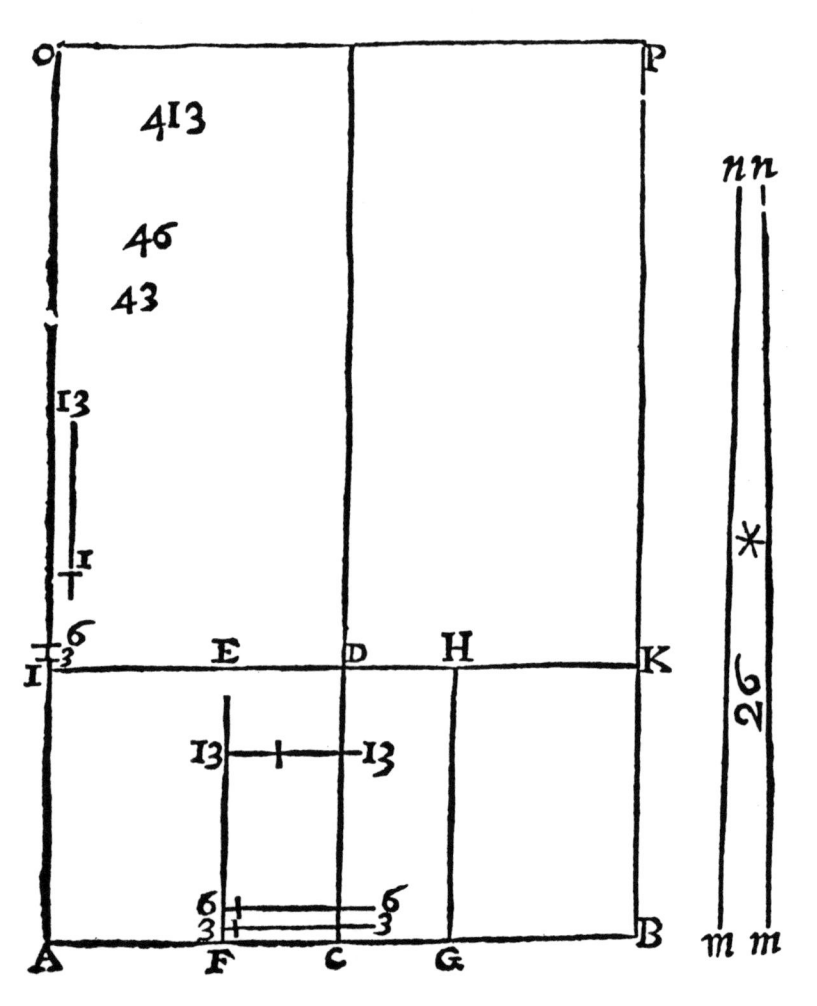

By this Propofition the Moulds being made and Sir-marked to the Body of the Veffel, and that they muft be marked, or ordered, to find the decreafe of her Bulks Body in the Mid fhips, and to come to her way abaft, that the Water may pafs to her Rudder to make her fteer, repair to the *Draught*, and firft fet off her Rifings thus: *Example*, We will begin at Timber 3 abaft, and his Rifing is 7 Inches: Therefore draw a Line parallel to the Bafe, or Ground-line *F G*, as the Line 3 3, 7 Inches from it, then take the Narrowing of the Floor with the Compaffes off, 3 alfo, and it is here 4 Inches, fhewed by the little Spot or Crofs in the Rifing-line 3 3, then feeking for the narrowing at the breadth for Timber 3, there is none, which fheweth that fhe keepeth the fame breadth at 3 ftill, 20 Foot; but feek for the height of the breadth, and it will lie higher at 3, than in the Mid-fhips by 6 Inches, fignified by the little Mark in the Line *A I*, a little above *I*, at the Point 3 ; then for the breadth at the top of the fide, find that at the top 3, in the Line *V W*, drawn to that end, and you will find that it is narrower there by 2 Foot 7 Inches, than at the breadth, or tumbleth home fo much at the height, 24 Foot fignified by an occult dark Line, drawn from the top of the Poop to the Fore-caftle, to order the height of the Head of the Top-timber Mould, anfwering to the narrowing of the fame at the Line *V W*; and this Point for 3 falls at the little Crofs-mark 3, in the upper part of the Figure. For the next *Example* we will fet off on our Platform the rifing Narrowings of Timber 6, and 6 rifeth from the Keel 1 Foot 7 Inches, as you fee the parallel Line 6 6 for breadth, the fame ftill at the breadth, but the height of the breadth is higher by 1 Foot, than at the Mid-fhip, fignified by the Mark at 6 in the Line: At the breadth, the Tumbling-home, 1 Foot 7 Inches and a half, at the height of 25 Foot 4 Inches, at the Point 6, and fo proceed of all the reft, beginning at 1, till you come aft to the fafhion Pieces; when you have fet off all the heights of Rifings, narrowings of the Floor, narrowings of the Breadth, height of the Breadth, at the Breadth of the Veffel, and alfo of the head of the Top-timber; then at each Point of the Floor ftick in a Nail, or a Gimblet, or fome fuch Thing; as fuppofe we begin here at 3, ftick one in the Mid-fhip-line at 3 ; another in the little Crofs, at the narrowing of the Floor at 3 ; another at the height of the breadth at 3 ; another at the little Crofs, as at the head of the Top-timber for 3 ; then, if you have a lower Futtock-mould, and an upper Futtock-mould, otherwife a naval Timber-mould and a Futtock-mould, nail them together with fmall Nails, and lay the Sir-marks of the Floor-mould and Futtock-mould, to the Gimblet that sticketh at the shortning of the Floor, for by this means the Floor-mould and Futtock-mould is haled downward; then make a Mark at the Crofs, in the Mid-ship Line C D, setting to the Mark of 3 for Timber 3, which will be the shortning of the Floor; then be sure the naval Timber-moulds touch the Gimblet at the breadth, and at the narrowing of the Floor, keeping the lower Sir-mark thereto; and make a Mark on the Futtock-mould, at the upper Gimblet, for the Rising alow lifteth up the Moulds higher; and if there be any crossing at the Foot of the naval Timber, and head of the Floor-mould, mark it, and set the Mark 3 to it, that you may know to lay them together again, and keeping the Futtock-mould fast lay to the top Timber-mould the breadth Sir-mark of the top Timber-mould, to the Gimblet at the breadth, so have you no more Sir-marks on the top Timber-mould but one, and guide the head of him till a Line stretched from the Crofs, at the head of the top Timber, compareth with the right part of top Timber-mould, then regard the crossing of the foot of the top Timber-mould, and the back of the Futtock, and mark it, setting the proper Mark 3 to it, that laying those Marks together, they may find their own places again, so having finished for this Room 3, take up the Moulds, and remove the Gimblets to the next, as to 6, here in our *Example*, and stick the Gimblets at all the Marks of 6; then lay down the Moulds again, laying down the Floor-mould to the Sir-mark of 6, on the narrowing of 6, and to the Gimblet, sticking on the Mid-ship-line of DC, and right on the same Line, at the crossing, make a Mark on the Floor-mould, which will be the narrowing of the Floor; then lay down the Futtock Mould, the Sir-mark on the foot to the Gimblet, on the narrowing of the Floor, and keeping the Mould to touch the Gimblets at both places, make a Mark for the breadth Sir-mark at 6, on the Futtock-mould, and set to it 6; then lay down the top Timber-mould, the breadth Sir-mark thereof to the Gimblet, sticking at the height of the breadth, that the back-side of the upper end may hang fair, by a right Line from the Crofs at the upper end of the top Timber at 6, by the back of the top Timber-mould, a strait Line may compare therewith, then keeping fast the Moulds so, till you have marked the crossing of the foot of the top Timber-mould, by the back of the Futtock, mark it on the foot of the top Timber-mould, and set it to the Mark of 6, so that when you are in any other place, as in the Woods a hewing of a Frame, where you hew to every place his Timber, you may be able to lay your Mould together, and mould it according to

your

The Compleat SHIP-WRIGHT.

your Draught. We will lay down the taking of one bend of Timbers more aft, where the breadth is narrowed, as at Timber 13, take his Rifing off, and meafure it by the Scale, and it will be 6 Foot 8 Inches, which fet off on your Platform, and draw thereto a parallel Line to the ground Line *AB*, as is the Line 13 13, then take off the narrowing of the Floor, as at 13, it is 2 Foot 2 Inches ; fet that off on the Line 13, from the Line *EF*, as at the little Crofs thereon, then take off the narrowing of the breadth at 13, and it will be 8 Inches ; draw therewith a little parallel Line, parallel to *IO*, as is the parallel Line 13 13, then feek the height of the breadth, as at 13, it will be from the upper edge of the Keel 12 Foot 3 Inches, and croffes the parallel Line at the lower end of it, juft then for the tumbling of the top Timber it will be 3 Foot 3 Inches, and at the height of 27 Foot 7 Inches, at the little Crofs 13. Now, for the order of the hollow Mould, the little round piece of an Arch, in the Scegg of the Veffel, there take off all the Rifings, and mark them on the Rifing-ftaff, on one edge, that they may be known from the other Rifings; as here, for Timber 13, take off the hollow Rifing, which will be at 1 Foot 10 Inches, fet it off on the rifing Staff, at 1 Foot 10 Inches from one end, and the Ufe of it will be in the Moulding; fet off the height of this hollow Rifing, on the middle Line of the Timber, when the Moulds are laid to pafs, and ftrike a Line from this Rifing, on the middle Line until it break off on the back of the Moulds, then lay the hollow Mould to the lower part of the breech of the Timber, and at the half breadth of the Keel, and fo bear in the other end till it juft touch the ftrait Line, made by the hollow Rifing, and the back of the Moulds ; and this mouldeth the lower part, or breech of the Timber, and bringeth in the hollow very fair : The fame Orders may be obferved afore, as abaft, on the other fide of the Moulds, and marked with Letters, to be known from them abaft. Then for the height of your Waals, you may make a Mark at every third or fourth Timber which you refolve to make frame Timbers ; I fay, you may make a Mark at every third or fourth Timber, for the height of the upper edge, or lower edge of the Waal, and fo bring on the Waal fair by thofe Marks on the one fide, and with a Level find the height of the other fide by the former.

Now I have briefly touched the Demonftration of a Ship by *Projection* ; I fhall now come to an *Arithmetical Way*, far furpaffing any Geometrical Demonftration for Exactnefs.

C 2 CHAP.

CHAP. VII.

Arithmetically shewing how to frame the Body of a Ship by Segments of Circles; being a true Way to examine the Truth of a Bow.

LET AB represent the length of a rising Line 12 Foot long, or 144 Inches, the height of it BC, 5 Foot or 60 Inches, to find the side DE, or DA, the Radius of the Circle AC, whereto AD is the Semidiameter; multiply the side AB 144 Inches in it self, and so cometh 20736, which Sum divide by the side BC, the height of the Rising 60 Inches, and so cometh 345, and $\frac{36}{60}$, which is abbreviated $\frac{3}{5}$; unto this 345⅗ must be added again the height of the Rising, BC, 60, which makes 405⅗ of an Inch, which is the whole Diameter of the Circle, the half whereof is 202½ Inches, and something more near ¼, therefore we will avoid the Fraction, and account 203 Inches, or 16 Foot 11 Inches, which is the length of the Sweep, or the side DE; and so in all other Sweeps given whatsoever, the Rule is general, and holds true in all things: As to find the Sweep at once, that will round any Beam, or other piece of Timber that is to be swept, remembring that, if it be a Beam, you are to find the Sweep but for half of its length.

    144
    144
    ———
    576
    576
    144
    ———
    20736

    2͞3 (3
  20736 (345
  6000
    66

Example: As, if the Beam be 30 Foot in length and to round one Foot, you must work by 15, the half length of the Beam; and turn 15 Foot into Inches, by multiplying 15 by 12, so cometh 180 Inches: Remember the length of the Rising-line if it be to find the Sweep, it must be multiplied by it self, or the half length of the Timber must be multiplied by it self, as 180 by 180, so cometh 32400, which must be divided by 12 the rounding, cometh in the Quotient 2700, to which must be added the 12 again, the rounding of the piece, and so it is 2712 the whole Diameter of the Circle, the half of this 2712 is 1356 for the length of the Sweep, or Semidiameter of the Circle, and so in all other Matters where the Sweep is required. This I read in Mr. *Gunter's* Book, where he calls it the half Chord, being given, and the versed Sine, to find the Diameter and Semidiameter of the Circle thereto belonging:

The Compleat SHIP-WRIGHT. 21

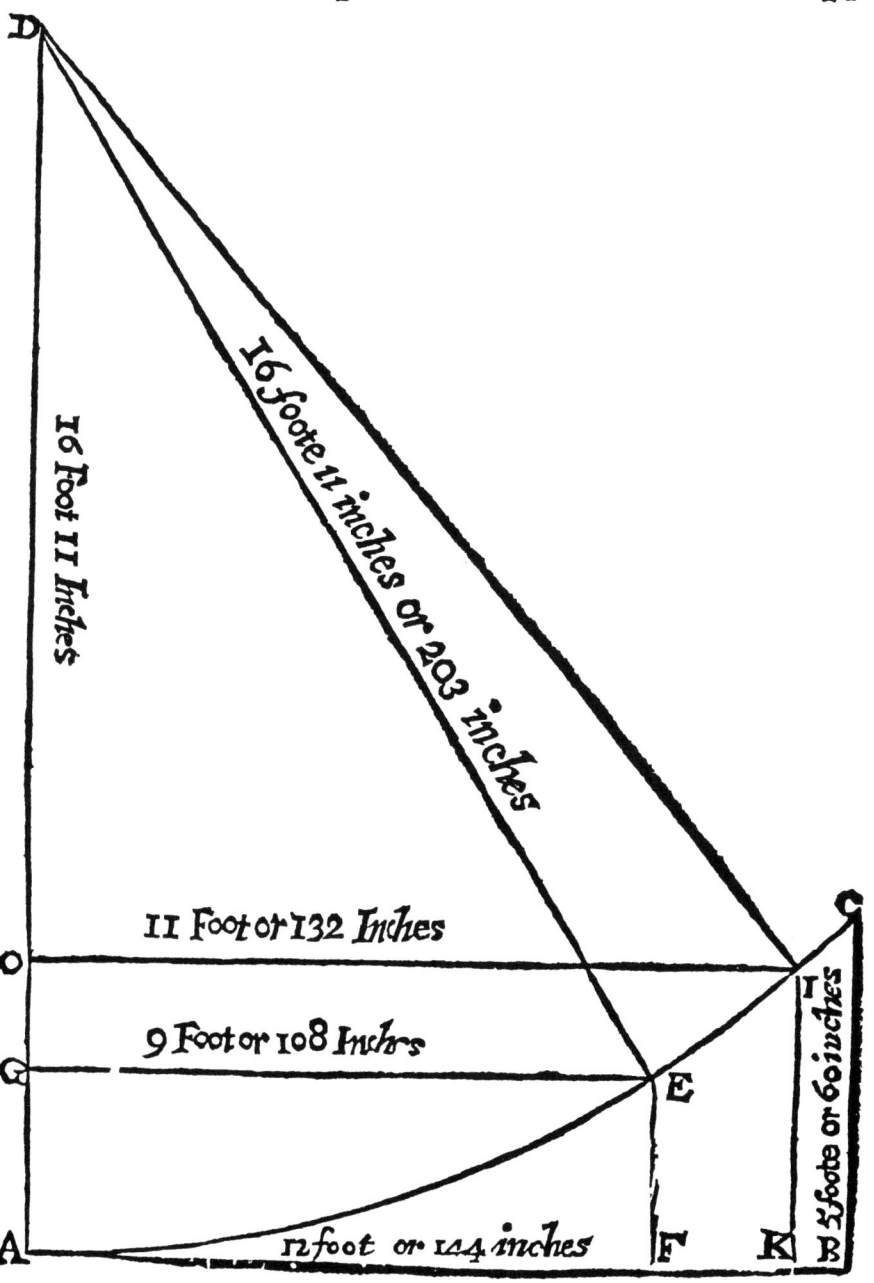

16 Foot 11 Inches

16 foote 11 inches or 203 inches

11 Foot or 132 Inches

9 Foot or 108 Inches

12 foot or 144 inches

5 foote or 60 inches

longing: Now this half Chord in our Work, is the length of the Rising-line, and the height of the rising on the Post is that in our Work, which he represents by the Name of the versed Sine; where remember to multiply the length of the Rising-line by it self, if it be a Rising-line, and divide by the height of the Rising, and to the Quotient add again the height of the Rising; so have you always the whole Diameter of the Circle; divide it by 2, so have you the length of the Sweep, or Semidiameter of the Circle.

Example in the Draught foregoing.

Where the length of the Rising-line is from the Point *E* to the Point *i*, 32 Foot; and a half the height thereof is the Line *D i*, 10 Foot: Turn both Sums into Inches, as 32 Foot multiplied by 12 produceth (adding the ½ Foot 6 Inches) 390 Inches length for the Rising-line: Then turn the height of the Rising into Inches, as 10 Foot multiplied by 12 produceth 120 Inches, from which 4 Inches must be subtracted, because of the dead Rising is 4 Inches, so then the height is 116 Inches: Now multiply the length 390 Inches by it self, makes 152100.

This Multiplication of the Sum 152100 must be divided by 116 Inches, the height of the Rising, and so cometh in the Quotient of the division 1311 Inches, unto this 1311 Inches must be added the 116 Inches, the height of the Rising $\frac{116}{1427}$, and it maketh 1427, which is the whole Diameter of the Circle; divide it by 2, to find the half of it, so have you in the Quotient 713 Inches ½ Inch for the length of the Sweep, which divided by 12, to bring it into Feet, maketh 59 Feet 5 Inches and a half; and so for all other circular Lines whatever, when the Length is known, and the rounding of them also known: As for the hanging of Waals, the height of them known in the Mid-ships from the Keel, subtracted from the height, at the Post, and that will be the hanging of them, which is the same with the height of the Rising-line on the Post, in the *Arithmetical* Work, and is the same with the versed Sine in *Geometry*. These, I think, Examples sufficient to signify the Construction of this way of working by Sweeps.

It followeth now, that I shew the Manner of finding the Risings of Timbers by *Arithmetick* also.

To find the Rising of the Line F E *in the Figure foregoing.*

The Sweep being first found to be as before 203 Inches, as the side D E signifieth, then there is known the side E G, 108 Inches; now these two sides being given, we are to find the third side D C, so here is made a right angled Triangle, two sides thereof are given to find a third, which to do proceed thus: Multiply the two sides given, by themselves, and subtract the Multiplication of the shortest side, from the Multiplication made of the other side, and extract the square Root of the Remainder, so have you the third side sought for.

Example in the following Triangle.

D

12 foote or 144 inches

A —————————————————— C
10 *foot or* 120 *Inches.*

Having the side D C, 12 Foot, which is 144 Inches, and the side A C, 10 Foot, otherwise 120 Inches; to find the side D A, multiply the sides given in themselves, which is called Squaring of them: As, multiply the side D C, 144 Inches by 144 Inches, so cometh 20736; then multiply the other side A C 120 also by it self, so cometh in the Quotient 14400, which must be subtracted from the other Multiplication, as you see, so cometh the Quotient 6336, from which the greatest Square must be extracted, called the Extraction of the square Root, which is 79 Inches, and almost another by the Fraction; that is, 6 Foot and very near 8 Inches.

144
144
―――
576
576
144
―――
20736

120
120
―――
000
240
120
―――
14400

20736
14400
―――
6336

Note,

Note, These Demonstrations, this and the former, are laid down by the first Scale, made to shew the Demonstration of a Scale in this Book at the Beginning.

Another Example.

So in the last Figure foregoing but one, the side *D E*, 203 Inches, which squared, or multiplied in it self, is 41209.

$$\begin{array}{r} 203 \\ 203 \\ \hline 609 \\ 000 \\ 406 \\ \hline 41209 \end{array}$$

Then the other side *G E*, 108, multiplied in it self, which is squaring of it, 11664, as you see.

$$\begin{array}{r} 108 \\ 108 \\ \hline 864 \\ 000 \\ 168 \\ \hline 11664 \end{array}$$

Which subtracted from the other Multiplication, as 11664 subtracted from 41209, resteth 29545, the square Root extracted from it, or the side of the greatest Square that can be taken from the Subtraction being found, is 171 and $\frac{1}{4}$, which 171 $\frac{1}{4}$, subtracted from 203: The length of the Sweep for one side resteth 31 Inches $\frac{1}{4}$, for the rising of the Line *E F*, and the like for any other Rising.

$$\begin{array}{r} 41209 \\ 11664 \\ \hline 29545 \end{array}$$

Another Example.

As at the Place *K I*, the Rising thereof is required, the side *D I* is as *D E*, 203 Inches.

Note, The length of the Sweep being found, always is one of the sides, in the finding the Rising of any Timber, and is always one of the Numbers, which when you have squared, note in a piece of Paper by it self, where you may always see what it is: So that in the finding of Rising, after the Sweep is found, all you

you have to do, is to know how many
Feet, or Inches, the Timber you seek for is
removed from the beginning, or Foot of the
Rising-line, which is the second side, and in
third *Example* it is 11 Foot or 132 Inches, *K I*
is from the Foot of the Line *A*, which squared
is 17424, which must be subtracted from the
Square made of Radius, which in the other
Example is 41209, and so resteth 23785, from
which extract the square Root, and it is 154 Inches and ¼, which subtracted from the length of
the Sweep, leaveth 48 Inches ¼, or 4 Foot and ¼
of an Inch, and so much is the Rising of the
said Timber, One *Example* in the *Draught*,
the length of that Sweep we found heretofore to
be 713 Inches, then we will seek to find the
Rising for Timber 13, standing aft from the
Point *E*, or foot of the Rising-line 324 Inches,
these are the given Sides: Then proceed,
square the Semidiameter of the Sweep 713, it maketh 508369;
then square the distance of the Timber 13, which is 324, and it
maketh 104976; these subtracted from the former Figures, resteth
403387, the square Root thereof is 635 ¼, nearest, which subtracted
from the Radius 713, resteth 77 Inches and ¼, or 6 Foot 5 Inches ¼,
which with 4 Inches Dead-rising, is 6 Foot 9 Inches ¼, and so
much is the rising of the Timber 13 from the Keel.

The square Root being of such great Use in Ship-building,
and some, tho' ingenious Workmen, not knowing how to perform
it, I have next inserted a Table of the square Root of all Numbers to 1690000, and the Squares of all Numbers to 1300.

Inch	Feet Inches	Squares	Inch	Feet Inches	Squares	Inch	Feet Inches	Squares
1	1	1	51	4 3	2601	101	8 5	10201
2	2	4	52	4 4	2704	102	8 6	10404
3	3	9	53	4 5	2809	103	8 7	10609
4	4	16	54	4 6	2916	104	8 8	10816
5	5	25	55	4 7	3025	105	8 9	11025
6	6	36	56	4 8	3136	106	8 10	11236
7	7	49	57	4 9	3249	107	8 11	11449
8	8	64	58	4 10	3364	108	9 00	11664
9	9	81	59	4 11	3481	109	9 1	11881
10	10	100	60	5 00	3600	110	9 2	12100
11	11	121	61	5 1	3721	111	9 3	12321
12	1 00	144	62	5 2	3844	112	9 4	12544
13	1 1	169	63	5 3	3969	113	9 5	12769
14	1 2	196	64	5 4	4096	114	9 6	12996
15	1 3	225	65	5 5	4225	115	9 7	13225
16	1 4	256	66	5 6	4356	116	9 8	13456
17	1 5	289	67	5 7	4489	117	9 9	13689
18	1 6	324	68	5 8	4624	118	9 10	13924
19	1 7	361	69	5 9	4761	119	9 11	14161
20	1 8	400	70	5 10	4900	120	10 00	14400
21	1 9	441	71	5 11	5041	121	10 1	14641
22	1 10	484	72	6 00	5184	122	10 2	14884
23	1 11	529	73	6 1	5329	123	10 3	15129
24	2 00	576	74	6 2	5476	124	10 4	15376
25	2 1	625	75	6 3	5625	125	10 5	15625
26	2 2	676	76	6 4	5776	126	10 6	15876
27	2 3	729	77	6 5	5929	127	10 7	16029
28	2 4	784	78	6 6	6084	128	10 8	16384
29	2 5	841	79	6 7	6241	129	10 9	16641
30	2 6	900	80	6 8	6400	130	10 10	16900
31	2 7	961	81	6 9	6561	131	10 11	17161
32	2 8	1024	82	6 10	6724	132	11 00	17424
33	2 9	1089	83	6 11	6889	133	11 1	17689
34	2 10	1156	84	7 00	7056	134	11 2	17956
35	2 11	1225	85	7 1	7225	135	11 3	18225
36	3 00	1296	86	7 2	7396	136	11 4	18496
37	3 1	1369	87	7 3	7569	137	11 5	18769
38	3 2	1444	88	7 4	7744	138	11 6	19044
39	3 3	1521	89	7 5	7921	139	11 7	19321
40	3 4	1600	90	7 6	8100	140	11 8	19600
41	3 5	1681	91	7 7	8281	141	11 9	19881
42	3 6	1764	92	7 8	8464	142	11 10	20164
43	3 7	1849	93	7 9	8649	143	11 11	20449
44	3 8	1936	94	7 10	8836	144	12 00	20736
45	3 9	2025	95	7 11	9025	145	12 1	21025
46	3 10	2116	96	8 00	9216	146	12 2	21416
47	3 11	2209	97	8 1	9409	147	12 3	21609
48	4 0	2304	98	8 2	9604	148	12 4	21904
49	4 1	2401	99	8 3	9801	149	12 5	22201
50	4 2	2500	100	8 4	10000	150	12 6	22500

27

In.F	Feet Inches	Squares	Inch	Feet Inches	Squares	Inch	Feet Inches	Squares
151	12 7	22801	201	16 9	40401	251	20 11	63001
152	12 8	23104	202	16 10	40844	252	21 00	63504
153	12 9	23409	203	16 11	41209	253	21 1	64009
154	12 10	23716	204	17 00	41616	254	21 2	64516
155	12 11	24025	205	17 1	42025	255	21 3	65025
156	13 00	24336	206	17 2	42436	256	21 4	65536
157	13 1	24649	207	17 3	42849	257	21 5	66049
158	13 2	24964	208	17 4	43264	258	21 6	66564
159	13 3	25381	209	17 5	43681	259	21 7	67081
160	13 4	25600	210	17 6	44100	260	21 8	67600
161	13 5	25921	211	17 7	44521	261	21 9	68121
162	13 6	26244	212	17 8	44944	262	21 10	68644
163	13 7	26569	213	17 9	45369	263	21 11	69169
164	13 8	26956	214	17 10	45796	264	22 00	69596
165	13 9	27225	215	17 11	46224	265	22 1	70425
166	13 10	27556	216	18 00	46656	266	22 2	70750
167	13 11	27886	217	18 1	47089	267	22 3	71289
168	14 00	28224	218	18 2	47524	268	22 4	71824
169	14 1	28561	219	18 3	47961	269	22 5	72361
170	14 2	28900	220	18 4	48400	270	22 6	72900
171	14 3	29241	221	18 5	48841	271	22 7	73441
172	14 4	29584	222	18 6	49284	272	22 8	73984
173	14 5	29929	223	18 7	49729	273	22 9	74529
174	14 6	30276	224	18 8	50176	274	22 10	74072
175	14 7	30625	225	18 9	50625	275	22 11	75575
176	14 8	31076	226	18 10	51076	276	23 00	76176
177	14 9	31329	227	18 11	51529	277	23 1	76729
178	14 10	31684	228	19 00	51984	278	23 2	77284
179	14 11	32041	229	19 1	52441	279	23 3	77841
180	15 0	32400	230	19 2	52900	280	23 4	78400
181	15 1	32761	231	19 3	53361	281	23 5	78961
182	15 2	33124	232	19 4	53824	282	23 6	79524
183	15 3	33488	233	19 5	54289	283	23 7	80089
184	15 4	33856	234	19 6	54656	284	23 8	80656
185	15 5	34025	235	19 7	55225	285	23 9	81225
186	15 6	34596	236	19 8	55696	286	23 10	81796
187	15 7	34969	237	19 9	56069	287	23 11	82369
188	15 8	35344	238	19 10	56644	288	24 00	82944
189	15 9	35721	239	19 11	57121	289	24 1	83521
190	15 10	36100	240	20 00	57600	290	24 2	84100
191	15 11	36481	241	20 1	58081	291	24 3	84681
192	16 00	36864	242	20 2	58564	292	24 4	85264
193	16 1	37249	243	20 3	59049	293	24 5	85849
194	16 2	37636	244	20 4	59536	294	24 6	86836
195	16 3	38025	245	20 5	60025	295	24 7	87025
196	16 4	38416	246	20 6	60516	296	24 8	87616
197	16 5	38809	247	20 7	61009	297	24 9	88209
198	16 6	39204	248	20 8	61504	298	24 10	88804
199	16 7	39601	249	20 9	62001	299	24 11	89401
200	16 8	40000	250	20 10	62500	300	25 00	90000

28

Inch	Feet Inches	Squares	Inch	Feet Inches	Squares	Inch	Feet Inches	Squares
301	25 1	90601	351	29 3	123206	401	33 5	160801
302	25 2	91204	352	29 4	123909	402	33 6	161604
303	25 3	91809	353	29 5	124604	403	33 7	162409
304	25 4	92416	354	29 6	125311	404	33 8	163216
305	25 5	93025	355	29 7	126025	405	33 9	164025
306	25 6	93636	356	29 8	126736	406	33 10	164836
307	25 7	94241	357	29 9	127449	407	33 11	165649
308	25 8	94864	358	29 10	128164	408	34 00	166464
309	25 9	95481	359	29 11	128881	409	34 1	167281
310	25 10	96100	360	30 00	129600	410	34 2	168100
311	25 11	96721	361	30 1	130321	411	34 3	168921
312	26 00	97344	362	30 2	131044	412	34 4	169744
313	26 1	97969	363	30 3	131779	413	34 5	170569
314	26 2	98596	364	30 4	132496	414	34 6	171396
315	26 3	99225	365	30 5	133225	415	34 7	172225
316	26 4	99856	366	30 6	133956	416	34 8	173056
317	26 5	100489	367	30 7	134689	417	34 9	173889
318	26 6	101124	368	30 8	135424	418	34 10	174724
319	26 7	101761	369	30 9	136161	419	34 11	175561
320	26 8	102400	370	30 10	136900	420	35 00	176400
321	26 9	103041	371	30 11	137640	421	35 1	177241
322	26 10	103684	372	31 00	138384	422	35 2	178084
323	26 11	104329	373	31 1	139129	423	35 3	178959
324	27 00	104976	374	31 2	139876	424	35 4	179776
325	27 1	105625	375	31 3	140625	425	35 5	180625
326	27 2	106276	376	31 4	141076	426	35 6	181476
327	27 3	106929	377	31 5	142129	427	35 7	182329
328	27 4	107584	378	31 6	142984	428	35 8	183184
329	27 5	108241	379	31 7	143641	429	35 9	184041
330	27 6	108900	380	31 8	144400	430	35 10	184900
331	27 7	109561	381	31 9	145161	431	35 11	185761
332	27 8	110224	382	31 10	145924	432	36 0	186624
333	27 9	110889	383	31 11	146689	433	36 1	187489
334	27 10	111556	384	32 00	147456	434	36 2	188356
335	27 11	112225	385	32 1	148225	435	36 3	189225
336	28 00	112896	386	32 2	149006	436	36 4	190096
337	28 1	113569	387	32 3	149769	437	36 5	190999
338	28 2	114244	388	32 4	150544	438	36 6	191044
339	28 3	114921	389	32 5	151321	439	36 7	192721
340	28 4	115600	390	32 6	152100	440	36 8	193600
341	28 5	116281	391	32 7	152881	441	36 9	194481
342	28 6	116964	392	32 8	153664	442	36 10	195364
343	28 7	117349	393	32 9	154440	443	36 11	196249
344	28 8	118336	394	32 10	155236	444	37 00	197136
345	28 9	119025	395	32 11	156025	445	37 1	198025
346	28 10	119716	396	33 00	156816	446	37 2	198916
347	28 11	120409	397	33 1	157609	447	37 3	199809
348	29 00	121104	398	33 2	158104	448	37 4	200704
349	29 1	121801	399	33 3	159201	449	37 5	201601
350	29 2	122500	400	33 4	160000	500	37 6	202509

29

Inch	Feet Inches	Squares	Inch	Feet Inches	Squares	Inch	Feet Inches	Squares
451	37 7	203401	501	41 9	251 01	551	45 11	303601
452	37 8	204304	502	41 10	252004	552	46 00	304704
453	37 9	205292	503	41 11	253009	553	46 1	305809
454	37 10	206116	504	42 00	254016	554	46 2	306916
455	37 11	207025	505	42 1	255025	555	46 3	308025
456	38 00	207936	506	42 2	256036	556	46 4	309136
457	38 1	208849	507	42 3	257049	557	46 5	310249
458	38 2	209764	508	42 4	258064	558	46 6	311364
459	38 3	210681	509	42 5	259081	559	46 7	312481
460	38 4	211600	510	42 6	260100	560	46 8	313600
461	38 5	212521	511	42 7	261121	561	46 9	314721
462	38 6	213444	512	42 8	262144	562	46 10	315844
463	38 7	214369	513	42 9	263169	563	46 11	316969
464	38 8	215296	514	42 10	264196	564	47 00	318096
465	38 9	216225	515	42 11	265225	565	47 1	319225
466	38 10	217156	516	43 00	266256	566	47 2	320356
467	38 11	218089	517	43 1	267289	567	47 3	321489
468	39 00	219024	518	43 2	268324	568	47 4	322624
469	39 1	219961	519	43 3	269361	569	47 5	323761
470	39 2	220900	520	43 4	270400	570	47 6	324900
471	39 3	221841	521	43 5	271441	571	47 7	326041
472	39 4	222784	522	43 6	272484	572	47 8	327184
473	39 5	223729	523	43 7	273529	573	47 9	328329
474	39 6	224676	524	43 8	274576	574	47 10	330276
475	39 7	225625	525	43 9	275625	575	47 11	330625
476	39 8	226576	526	43 10	276676	576	48 00	331776
477	39 9	227429	527	43 11	277729	577	48 1	332929
478	39 10	228484	528	44 00	278784	578	48 2	334084
479	39 11	229141	529	44 1	280241	579	48 3	335241
480	40 00	230400	530	44 2	280900	580	48 4	336400
481	40 1	231361	531	44 3	281961	581	48 5	337561
482	40 2	232324	532	44 4	284024	582	48 6	338724
483	40 3	233289	533	44 5	285089	583	48 7	340089
484	40 4	234256	534	44 6	285156	584	48 8	341056
485	40 5	235225	535	44 7	286225	585	48 9	342225
486	40 6	236196	536	44 8	287296	586	48 10	343396
487	40 7	237169	537	44 9	288369	587	48 11	344669
488	40 8	238144	538	44 10	290444	588	49 00	345744
489	40 9	239121	539	44 11	290521	589	49 1	346921
490	40 10	240100	540	45 00	291600	590	49 2	348100
491	40 11	240981	541	45 1	292681	591	49 3	349281
492	41 00	242064	542	45 2	293764	592	49 4	350464
493	41 1	243049	543	45 3	294849	593	49 5	351649
494	41 2	244036	544	45 4	295936	594	49 6	352836
495	41 3	245025	545	45 5	297025	595	49 7	353925
496	41 4	246016	546	45 6	298016	596	49 8	354216
497	41 5	246009	547	45 7	299209	597	49 9	355409
498	41 6	247004	548	45 8	300307	598	49 10	356604
499	41 7	249001	549	45 9	301401	599	49 11	358801
500	41 8	250000	550	45 10	302500	600	50 00	460000

30

Inch	Feet Inches	Squares	Inch	Feet Inches	Squares	Inch	Feet Inches	Squares
601	50 1	361201	651	54 3	423801	701	58 5	491401
602	50 2	362404	652	54 4	425104	702	58 6	492804
603	50 3	363609	653	54 5	426409	703	58 7	494209
604	50 4	364816	654	54 6	427716	704	58 8	495616
605	50 5	366025	655	54 7	429025	705	58 9	497025
606	50 6	367236	656	54 8	430336	706	58 10	498436
607	50 7	368449	657	54 9	431449	707	58 11	498849
608	50 8	369664	658	54 10	432969	708	59 00	501264
609	50 9	370881	659	54 11	434181	709	59 1	502681
610	50 10	372100	660	55 00	435600	710	59 2	504100
611	50 11	373321	661	55 1	436921	711	59 3	505525
612	51 00	374544	662	55 2	438244	712	59 4	506944
613	51 1	375769	663	55 3	439569	713	59 5	508669
614	51 2	376996	664	55 4	440896	714	59 6	509796
615	51 3	378225	665	55 5	442225	715	59 7	511225
616	51 4	379456	666	55 6	443556	716	59 8	512656
617	51 5	380689	667	55 7	444889	717	59 9	514089
618	51 6	381924	668	55 8	446224	718	59 10	515824
619	51 7	383161	669	55 9	447561	719	59 11	516961
620	51 8	384400	670	55 10	448900	720	60 00	518400
621	51 9	385641	671	55 11	450241	721	60 1	519841
622	51 10	386884	672	56 00	451544	722	60 2	521284
623	51 11	388129	673	56 1	452829	723	60 3	522729
624	52 00	389376	674	56 2	454276	724	60 4	524175
625	52 1	390625	675	56 3	455625	725	60 5	525625
626	52 2	391876	676	56 4	456976	726	60 6	526976
627	52 3	393129	677	56 5	458329	727	60 7	528529
628	52 4	394384	678	56 6	459684	728	60 8	529984
629	52 5	395641	679	56 7	461041	729	60 9	521421
630	52 6	396900	680	56 8	462400	730	60 10	522900
631	52 7	398161	681	56 9	463761	731	60 11	524361
632	52 8	399424	682	56 10	465124	732	61 00	535844
633	52 9	400489	683	56 11	466489	733	61 1	537289
634	52 10	401956	684	57 00	467856	734	61 2	538656
635	52 11	403225	685	57 1	469225	735	61 3	540225
636	53 00	404496	686	57 2	470596	736	61 4	541656
637	53 1	405769	687	57 3	471939	737	61 5	543169
638	53 2	407044	688	57 4	473344	738	61 6	544644
639	53 3	408321	689	57 5	475721	739	61 7	546031
640	53 4	409600	690	57 6	476700	740	61 8	547600
641	53 5	410881	691	57 7	477841	741	61 9	549081
642	53 6	412164	692	57 8	478864	742	61 10	550564
643	53 7	413449	693	57 9	480269	743	61 11	552049
644	53 8	414736	694	57 10	481656	744	62 00	553436
645	53 9	416025	695	57 11	482825	745	62 1	555025
646	53 10	417316	696	58 00	484416	746	62 2	556515
647	53 11	418609	697	58 1	485809	747	62 3	558009
648	54 00	429904	698	58 2	487204	748	62 4	559504
649	54 1	421201	699	58 3	488601	749	62 5	561001
650	54 2	422500	700	58 4	490000	750	62 6	562500

Inch	Feet Inches	Squares	Inch	Feet Inches	Squares	Inch	Squares
751	62 7	564001	801	66 9	641601	851	724201
752	62 8	565504	802	66 10	642204	852	725904
753	62 9	567009	803	66 11	644809	853	727609
754	62 10	568516	804	67 00	646416	854	729216
755	62 11	570025	805	67 1	648025	855	731025
756	63 00	571536	806	67 2	649836	856	732736
757	63 1	573049	807	67 3	651249	857	734449
758	63 2	574564	808	67 4	652864	858	736164
759	63 3	576081	809	67 5	654481	859	737681
760	63 4	577600	810	67 6	656100	860	739600
761	63 5	579121	811	67 7	657721	861	741321
762	63 6	580644	812	67 8	659344	862	743044
763	63 7	582169	813	67 9	660969	863	744769
764	63 8	583696	814	67 10	662596	864	746396
765	63 9	585225	815	67 11	664225	865	748225
766	63 10	586756	816	68 00	665856	866	749956
767	63 11	588289	817	68 1	667429	867	753689
768	64 00	589824	818	68 2	669124	868	753824
769	64 1	591361	819	68 3	671771	869	755161
770	64 2	592900	820	68 4	672400	870	756900
771	64 3	594441	821	68 5	674041	871	758641
772	64 4	595984	822	68 6	675684	872	760384
773	64 5	597529	823	68 7	677329	873	762129
774	64 6	599076	824	68 8	678976	874	763776
775	64 7	600625	825	68 9	680625	875	765625
776	64 8	602176	826	68 10	682276	876	767376
777	64 9	604729	827	68 11	684129	877	769129
778	64 10	606284	828	69 00	685584	878	770884
779	64 11	607841	829	69 1	688241	879	772641
780	65 00	608400	830	69 2	688900	880	774400
781	65 1	609961	831	69 3	689661	881	777161
782	65 2	611524	832	69 4	691224	882	777924
783	65 3	613099	833	69 5	693889	883	779589
784	65 4	614656	834	69 6	695556	884	781456
785	65 5	616225	835	69 7	697225	885	783225
786	65 6	617796	835	69 8	698896	886	784996
787	65 7	619369	837	69 9	700169	887	786769
788	65 8	620944	838	69 10	702244	888	788544
789	65 9	622521	839	69 11	703921	889	790321
790	65 10	624100	840	70 00	705600	890	792100
791	65 11	625681	841	70 1	707281	891	793881
792	66 00	627964	842	70 2	708964	892	795664
793	66 1	628849	843	70 3	710649	893	797449
794	66 2	630456	844	70 4	711336	894	799236
795	66 3	632125	845	70 5	714025	895	801025
796	66 4	633616	846	70 6	715716	896	802816
797	66 5	635209	847	70 7	717309	897	804609
798	66 6	637404	848	70 8	719004	898	805904
799	66 7	638401	849	70 9	720801	899	808201
800	66 8	640000	850	70 10	722500	900	810000

Inch	Squares	Inch	Squares	Inch	Squares	Inch	Squares
901	811801	951	904401	1001	1002001	1051	1104601
902	813604	952	906304	1002	1004004	1052	1106704
903	815409	953	908209	1003	1006009	1053	1108809
904	817216	954	910116	1004	1008016	1054	1110916
905	819025	955	912025	1005	1010025	1055	1113025
906	820836	956	913936	1006	1012036	1056	1115136
907	822649	957	915849	1007	1014049	1057	1117249
908	824464	958	917764	1008	1016064	1058	1119364
909	826281	959	919681	1009	1018081	1059	1120489
910	828100	960	921600	1010	1020100	1060	1123600
911	829921	961	923521	1011	1022121	1061	1125721
912	831741	962	925444	1012	1024104	1062	1127844
913	833569	963	928369	1013	1026169	1063	1129969
914	835369	964	929296	1014	1028196	1064	1132096
915	837225	965	931225	1015	1030225	1055	1134225
916	839056	966	933256	1016	1032256	1066	1136358
917	840789	967	935089	1017	1034289	1067	1138489
918	842724	968	937024	1018	1036324	1068	1140624
919	844561	969	939961	1019	1038361	1069	1142761
920	846400	970	940900	1020	1040400	1070	1144900
921	847241	971	942741	1021	1042441	1071	1147041
922	850084	972	944784	1022	1044284	1072	1149184
923	851929	973	946729	1023	1046529	1073	1151329
924	853746	974	948676	1024	1048576	1074	1153476
925	855625	975	950625	1025	1050625	1075	1155625
926	857476	976	952576	1026	1052676	1076	1157976
927	859329	977	954529	1027	1054729	1077	1159929
928	861184	978	956484	1028	1056784	1078	1162074
929	863041	979	958441	1029	1058841	1079	1164241
930	864900	980	960400	1030	1060900	1080	1166400
931	866761	981	962361	1031	1062961	1081	1168561
932	868624	982	964324	1032	1065024	1082	1170724
933	870489	983	966289	1033	1067089	1083	1172889
934	872356	984	968256	1034	1069156	1084	1175056
935	874225	985	970225	1035	1071225	1085	1177225
936	876096	986	972196	1036	1073296	1086	1179396
937	877869	987	974169	1037	1075369	1087	1181569
938	879844	988	976144	1038	1077444	1088	1183744
939	881721	989	978121	1039	1079521	1089	1185921
940	883600	990	980100	1040	1081600	1090	1188100
941	885481	991	982081	1041	1082681	1091	1190281
942	886364	992	984064	1042	1085764	1092	1192464
943	889249	993	986049	1043	1087849	1093	1194649
944	881136	994	988036	1044	1089936	1094	1196836
945	893025	995	990025	1045	1092025	1095	1199025
946	894916	996	992016	1046	1094106	1096	1201216
947	896809	997	994009	1047	1096209	1097	1203409
948	898704	998	996004	1048	1098304	1098	1205604
949	900601	999	998001	1049	1100401	1099	1207801
950	902500	1000	1000000	1050	1102500	1100	1210000

Inch	Squares	Inch	Squares	Inch	Squares	Inch	Squares
1101	1212201	1151	1324801	1201	1442401	1251	1565001
1102	1214404	1152	1327104	1202	1444804	1252	1567504
1103	1216609	1153	1329409	1203	1447209	1253	1570009
1104	1218816	1154	1331716	1204	1449616	1254	1572416
1105	1221025	1155	1334025	1205	1452025	1255	1575021
1106	1223396	1156	1336336	1206	1454436	1256	1577536
1107	1225449	1157	1338649	1207	1456849	1257	1580049
1108	1227664	1158	1340964	1208	1459264	1258	1582564
1109	1229881	1159	1343381	1209	1461681	1259	1585081
1110	1232100	1160	1345600	1210	1464100	1260	1587600
1111	1234321	1161	1347921	1211	1466521	1261	1590021
1112	1236544	1162	1350244	1212	1468944	1262	1592644
1113	1238769	1163	1352569	1213	1471369	1263	1595169
1114	1240969	1164	1354396	1214	1473796	1264	1597706
1115	1242625	1165	1357225	1215	1476225	1265	1600225
1116	1245459	1166	1358556	1216	1478656	1266	1602756
1117	1247689	1167	1361689	1217	1480989	1267	1605289
1118	1249924	1168	1364124	1218	1483924	1268	1607824
1119	1252161	1169	1366921	1219	1485961	1269	1609361
1120	1254400	1170	1368900	1220	1488400	1270	1612900
1121	1256641	1171	1371240	1221	1490841	1271	1615441
1122	1258884	1172	1373584	1222	1493244	1272	1617984
1123	1261029	1173	1375929	1223	1495729	1273	1620529
1124	1263376	1174	1378276	1224	1498246	1274	1622076
1125	1265625	1175	1380625	1225	1500125	1275	1625625
1126	1267876	1176	1382979	1226	1503076	1276	1628176
1127	1270029	1177	1383329	1227	1505529	1277	1630729
1128	1272384	1178	1387684	1228	1507984	1278	1633464
1129	1274641	1179	1390041	1229	1510441	1279	1635841
1130	1276900	1180	1392400	1230	1512900	1280	1638400
1131	1279161	1181	1394761	1231	1515361	1281	1640961
1132	1281434	1182	1397124	1232	1517824	1282	1643524
1133	1283689	1183	1399489	1233	1520289	1283	1645989
1134	1285956	1184	1401156	1234	1522656	1284	1645656
1135	1288225	1185	1404225	1235	1525225	1285	1651225
1136	1287496	1186	1406606	1236	1527696	1286	1653796
1137	1292769	1187	1408904	1237	1530169	1287	1656369
1138	1294994	1188	1411124	1238	1534224	1288	1658944
1139	1297321	1189	1413711	1239	1535121	1289	1661521
1140	1299640	1190	1416100	1240	1537600	1290	1664100
1141	1301881	1191	1418481	1241	1540081	1291	1666681
1142	1304164	1192	1420864	1242	1542564	1292	1669264
1143	1306449	1193	1423249	1243	1545049	1293	1671849
1144	1308736	1194	1425639	1244	1547536	1294	1674336
1145	1311025	1195	1428025	1245	1550025	1295	1677025
1146	1313316	1196	1430416	1246	1552516	1296	1679616
1147	1315509	1197	1432809	1247	1555009	1297	1682209
1148	1317904	1198	1435204	1248	1557504	1298	1683804
1149	1320201	1199	1437601	1249	1560001	1299	1687401
1150	1322500	1200	1440000	1250	1562500	1300	1690000

E   CHAP.

CHAP. VIII.

How to extract the Square Root, and compose the foregoing Table of Squares.

KNow then that a Square Number hath its sides equal every way as are the sides of 4 represented by ∷ Pricks. And you see that every way of all the 4 sides it containeth 2, and so 2 times 2, make 4, which is the squaring of a Number; so you see 9 Pricks is a Square, or 9 is a square Number, whose side is 3; and 3 times 3 make 9, but 2 times 3 is not a square Number, as you see ⦂⦂⦂, being but 2 one way, and the other way 3, that make but 6, so then all the Numbers between 4 and 9, are not square Numbers: By the like reason, a Square made of the next square Number is 16; for 4 times 4 is 16, as by the Pricks you may see it represented here, every of the 4 sides containing 4, make a squared Number of 16, and all the Numbers that are between 9 and 16, as 2 times 4, or 3 times 4, are not Squares, but have a Fraction annexed to them; so also any Number between 16 and 25, are not Squares, as 4 times 5, or 2 times 5, or 3 times 5; these are not square Numbers; but 5 times 5 is a squared Number, and maketh 25, where note, that to square a Number, and to extract the square Root, is two different things; for when we say, to square a Number, it is to multiply it in it self, or by it self; or when we say, or speak of a Number squared, it is a Number multiplied in it self; but to extract the square Root, is to find the side of the Square in a Number given, or the extracted square Root is the square Root found in any given Number.

Thus you may conceive of the Squares of 6, for 6 times 6 make 36; 7 times 7 is 49; 8 times 8 make 64; 9 times 9 make 81; 10 times 10 make 100: There is all the Squares made of the 9 Figures, expressed by this little Table annexed, as against each Figure is the Square made of them, as 2 times 2 is 4; so is 4 against 2, as you see.

1	1
2	4
3	9
4	16
5	25
6	36
7	49
8	64
9	81
10	100

Now

The Compleat SHIP-WRIGHT.

Now to extract the square Root from greater Numbers, as from 144, proceed thus, write down the Sum given as followeth, and make a Quotient on the Right-hand, as you see, and set Pricks under every other Figure, beginning at the Right-hand, and set Pricks towards the Left-hand, under every other Figure, so in this Number 144 consisting of three Figures, there is two Pricks, and so many Figures must the Quotient consist of; then begin at the Left-hand of the Sum, and say, or inquire for the greatest Square in the Figure or Figures, over the first Prick, at the Left-hand, which, here, is but 1, therefore you can take but 1, for 1 is always the Square, or Cube of 1; therefore write 1 in the Quotient, and subtract that 1 from the 1 over the Left-hand Prick, and cancel it, nothing remaining, write a Cypher over it, as you see, so have you one Figure of the Quotient, then double your Figure found in the Quotient, as 2 times 1 is 2; write that 2 under the Figure between the next Pricks, which is the Divisor for the second Figure, then say, how many times 2 can I have in 4, over the Divisor? I say 2, therefore I write 2 in the Quotient, saying, 2 times 2 is 4, which subtract from the 4 over head, cancel the Divisor, and the 4 over head, and write a Cypher over it, then square the last Figure found in the Quotient, saying 2 times 2 is 4, which subtract from the 4 over the Prick, and so resteth 0, therefore cancel the 4 and write Cyphers over head, signifying that the Number given to find the Root of, is a just square Number, the Root or Side is 12, the Proof hereof is by Multiplication of the Quotient in it self, as 12 by 12 make 144, which if it be the same with the Sum given to be extracted, it is rightly done; if it do not agree, it is not true.

144 (

0
144 (1

000
144 (12
·2·

Example of another Sum.

Let 625 be given to find the square Root of it, write down the Sum, make a Quotient, and set Pricks under every other Figure, then inquire for the greatest Square in the Figure, over the Prick, at the Left-hand; I say 2 is the greatest Square can be taken, for 3 times 3 is 9, and here the Figure is but 6; so I write 2 in the Quotient, and square it, saying, 2 times 2 is 4, taken from 6, so resteth 2; I cancel the 6, and write 2 over it, as you see, then double the Figure in the Quotient

2
625 (2
· ·

2
625 (2
·4·

tient, saying 2 times 2 is 4; this 4 is the second Divisor, I write it between the two next Pricks, and say how many times 4 can I have in 22? and I find 5 times; for 5 times 4 is 20, taken from 22, the Figures over 4, so resteth 2; therefore I write 5 in the Quotient, and saying, 5 times 4 make 20; therefore I cancel the 4 Divisor, and the 22, and write 2 over head, then square the last Figure found, 5 by 5 make 25, taken from 25 over head, resteth nothing, so the Number given is a square Number.

  22 . .
  625 (25
  ·4·

  22
  625 (25
  ·4·

 A Sum of 5476, given to find the nearest square Root in it, write down the Sum, and make a Quotient and prick underneath, as afore shewed; say, What is the greatest Square in the Figure over the Left-hand Prick? and I find it to be 7, for 7 times 7 make 49, but 8 times 8 make 64, 10 too much, therefore I write 7 in the Quotient, and take 7 times 7, that is, 49 from 54, so resteth 5, which I write over the Prick, and cancel the 5 and the 4; then I double the Figure in the Quotient, which maketh 14 for the Divisor; I write the first Figure of the Divisor, if there be more than 1 under the Figure, between the two next Pricks, and all the other Figures in their places towards the Left-hand; then inquire how many times can 1 be taken from 5, over head, and I find it may be taken four times; I write therefore 4 in the Quotient, and say, 4 times 1 is 4, from 5, so resteth 1: I cancel the 1 and 5, and write 1 over the 5, then I say, 4 times 4 make 16, from 17 resteth 1 : I cancel the 4 Divisor, and write 1 over 7, and cancel the other 1 and the 7; then I square the last Figure found, for so it must be at every Prick, 4 times 4 make 16, which I subtract from the 16 over the last Prick, and so I see nothing remaineth : That sheweth the Sum given to be a just square Sum.

  5
  5476 (7
  · ·

  1
  51
  5476 (74
  · ·
  14

  0
  510
  5476 (74
  · ·
  14

Example of another Sum.

 As if 528563 be given to find the greatest side of the Square therein, I write down the Sum as followeth, and make the Quotient, and set the Pricks under every other Figure as you see; and seeing there is 3 Pricks, it telleth, that there must be 3 Figures in the Quotient, then beginning at the Figures, over the Left-hand Prick, I take the greatest

Square

The Compleat SHIP-WRIGHT.   37

Square in 52, and I find it 7, for 7 times 7 make 49; therefore I write down 7 in the Quotient, and subtract 49 from 52, so resteth 3, therefore cancel the 52, and write 3 over the 2, as you see; then double the Quotient 7, it maketh 14, for a new Divisor, which write down, the first Figure thereof under the Figure between the two next Pricks, namely 4 under 8, and the other Figure of the Divisor one place further to the Left-hand, under the 3, as you see; then take the Divisor 1, as many times as you can, from the Figure 3 over head, so as that after the Division be made, there may be the Square of the last Figure of the Quotient, taken from the Figures over the next Prick, as I can take 1 but 2 times from 2; therefore I write 2 in the Quotient, and cancel the Divisor 1, saying, 2 times 1 is 2, from 3; so resteth 1 : I cancel the Figure 3 also, and write 1 over head, as you see: Then 2 times 4 is 8, from 8 over head resteth nothing; therefore I cancel the second Figure of the Divisor, 4 and 8, and write a Cypher over 8, as you see; then the next place being a Prick, I must square the last Figure found, saying, 2 times 2 make 4, from 5; the Figure over the Prick resteth 1, as you see; therefore I cancel the 5, and write 1 over it, as you see, and here is a Fraction of 101.

    Then for a new Divisor, double the Quotient 72, and it makes 144, which is a new Divisor, the first Figure thereof write under the Figure between the next Pricks, as the first 4 under 6 in the Sum; and the other Figures toward the Left-hand, in the order as you see : Then how many times 1 in 10 over head, and I see I cannot take 8 times, for that there will not be left to take out the other Figures from, nor for the Square of the last Figure, which if were 8 would be 64 from the Figure over the Prick, therefore I take but 7, for by a light Examination I see that will do, therefore I write down 7 in the Quotient, and proceed to the Division thus, 7 times 1 is 7, from 10 over head remaineth 3, which I write down, and cancel the 10, as you see; then 7 times 4 is 28, from 31 over head, so

    3
528563 (7
· · ·

    3
528563 (7
· · ·
  14

  1
 30
528563 (72
· · ·
 14

  1
 301
528563 (727
· · ·
 14

  1
 301
528563 (727
· · ·
 144
  14

 131
 301
528563 (727
· · ·
 144
  14   re-

38 — *The Compleat* SHIP-WRIGHT.

remaineth 3, which I alſo write down, and cancel the 31, then again 7 times 4, the other Figure of the Diviſor, is alſo 28, which taken from 36 over head, reſteth 8, which I write down over 6, and ſo cancel the 36, and then the Sum ſtandeth as you ſee.

Then, laſtly, ſquare the laſt Figure of the Quotient, 7 times 7 make 49, taken from 83, the Figures over the Prick, reſteth 34, as a Fraction, and the Sum is finiſhed: But in regard here is a Fraction, by that it tells you that the Sum given was no ſquare Number; and the greateſt Square therein is 727, the Proof is by Multiplication adding in the Fraction thus, 727 multiplied by 727, make 528529, then adding in the Fraction of 34 maketh it 528563, the juſt Sum given.

But ſome may object, and ſay, that this is a very tedious way of Work, and will take up a great deal of time. It is ture, it is more Labour than Demonſtration, but the truth of it might very well plead for Patience to work it; but it is not neceſſary you perform all the Parts by it, that is in every Particular as the exact hanging of the Waal at every Timber, but it may ſuffice at every third or fourth Timber, to find the hanging of the Waals, only the Riſings alow, afore and abaft, I would work to every Timber there.

But to make it more brief, in the foregoing Table of Squares, the Numbers are contrived to the ſame purpoſe, to avoid the tedious Extraction of the Root, and only uſe Addition and Subtraction, being but a very little difference between the finding the Riſings by this Table, and by the *Draught*; for in this kind of *Arithmetical* Work, it mattereth not, whether there be any *Draught* drawn at all, or no, if the Builder only note in his Book the length by the Keel, and the breadth at the Beam, the Rack of the Stem, Rack of the Poſt, depth of the Water to ſail in, depth of the Hold, height of the Waals abaft, afore at the Mid-ſhips, and all the remarkable things to be noted, he may be able to build a Veſſel, and never draw a *Draught* at all, and yet affirm his Work to be abſolutely true according to Art, and a great deal more exact than by *Draught*. The Uſe of the Table follows.

CHAP.

CHAP. IX.

The Description and Use of the Table of SQUARES.

TO save the Practitioner a Labour of extracting of Roots, for here they are ready done to thy hand of purpose, and all the Use of *Arithmetick* required is only Subtraction, as *Example* in the Figure of the Sweep foregoing, being found to be 203 Inches, as you saw it found before, which is, I say, always one side of the Triangle, made of the Side *D I*, then knowing the length of *O I*, 132 Inches, which is the distance of the Point, of which the Risings is sought at; seek in the Tables, under the Title of *Inches*, at the head of the Tables, for 132, you will find it in the first Page and in the third Column towards the Left-hand, and the twenty-second Line; and right-against it, in the same Line under the next Title of *Squares*, you have 17424, the Square made of 132, which subtract from the Square made of 203, which is 41209, which is found in the second Page of the Tables, in the sixth Column and the third Line: So resteth 23785; seek the Number nearest to it in the Table, under the Title of *Square*, which you will find in the second Page, fourth Line, you find not just the same Number, for instead of 23785, you find 23716, too little by 59, and the Root answering thereto is in the same Line, under the Title of *Inches*, towards the Left-hand, which is 154; now if you take the next Square lower to the Left-hand, fifth Line, it is 24025, 250 too much, so you may see it is nearer to the fourth Line, because there it was too little but by 59, so that you may see it will be $\frac{1}{4}$ of an Inch less than the Number of Inches belonging to the fifth Line, and about $\frac{1}{4}$ of an Inch more than the Numbers in the fourth Line: So that you see it is answered, the third Side *D O* is 154, and $\frac{1}{4}$ of an Inch, which subtracted from the whole Sweep 203 leaveth 48 $\frac{1}{4}$ Inches for the Rising, so you have no need of Extraction of the Roots by these Tables, it is already done to your hand. The Column that is between the *Inches* and the *Squares*, and written *Feet Inches* in the Head, is to shew you how many Feet and Inches of the Foot any Number of Inches is; as here the Number 203 Inches sought, and found in the Tables, in the second Page, and third Line, just against it, in the same Line, between that and the *Squares*, is 16 ——— 11: Shewing that it is 16 Feet and

11 Inches; or if the Square were given, as 41209, found at the second Page and third Line, and the sixth Column, you have 16 Feet 11 Inches, and if you seek for it in *Inches*, in the fourth Column and same Line, you have 203 Inches. Thus it is very ready to reduce Inches into Feet Measure, or Feet into Inches.

Another Example.

In the same Figure, to find the Rising at the Point *F*, the Sweep being 203 Inches, as before is said, is always one side, throughout the whole Work of the same Rising-line whose *Square* is 41209, as is found in the second Page, the third Line, the other side from the Point *A F*, is 9 Foot or 108 Inches, whose *Square* is 11664, found in the first Page and the twenty-eighth Line; now subtract the Square made of the side *A F*, 11664, from the Square of the side *D E*, so remaineth 29545.

    41209
    11664
    ———
    29545

Seek in the Table of *Squares* for that Number, and I find in the second Page and twenty-second Line, the third Column, 29584, the nearest Number to it, yet it is a little too much, near the ¼ of an Inch; and toward the Left-hand in the same Line, the next Column under the Title *Feet Inches*, you find 14; 4 signifying that to be 14 Feet 4 Inches: And in one Column more to the Left-hand, and the same Line, you see under the Title of *Inches* 172, over the head you tituled *Inches*, which must be subtracted from 203 Inches, so remaineth 31 Inches for the Rising of *F E*, which is 2 Foot 7 Inches, as in the first Page of the Table, and in the thirty-first Line.

    203
    172
    ———
    031

These few *Examples*, I think, may be sufficient to shew the Use of the foregoing Tables of the Squares, the Benefit whereof may be very great, for such as shall make Use of the same. If any desire the finding of the Fractions of these Squares, when he findeth not his just Figures in the *Squares*, let him do thus, subtract the Figures under his Number from the Figures above his Number, the Remainder shall be the Denominator, then from these Figures given, subtract the Remainder from the next *Squares* less, the Remainder shall be the Numerator to that Fraction.

As for *Example*, in the foregoing Figures, after Subtraction, there remains 29545; the nearest agreeing in the Tables, is 29584, the next lesser Square Number in the Table is 29241, which is more a great deal too little, than the other is too great; then subtract the lesser square Number 29241, from 29584, and so resteth 343, which must be the Denominator, then again from the true Number given 29545 subtract the next lesser square Number in the Table 29241, and so there resteth after Subtraction 304, which is the Numerator to the Fraction, and must be thus written $\frac{304}{343}$: So then the Number belonging to 29584, is 171 Inches and $\frac{304}{343}$ parts of one Inch, which being abbreviated, is something more than $\frac{1}{4}$ of an Inch, and not full $\frac{7}{8}$ of one Inch.

$$\begin{array}{r} 29584 \\ 29241 \\ \hline 343 \end{array}$$

Thus, he that pleaseth, may find the rising of any Timber, or narrowing of any Place by these Tables and the help of Subtraction, exactly to any Circle whatsoever, but it may suffice, that a Man, going to his Tables, may see which *Square* his Figures have greatest Affinity with, and may estimate the Difference near enough without seeking for the Fraction, which will easily be known by Practice.

CHAP. X.

Shewing how to hang a Rising-line by several Sweeps, to make it rounder aftward, than at the beginning of the same.

IF any be desirous to have a Rising-line rounder aftward than it is at the fore-part of it, they must proceed thus: First, work by the Sweep that they would have first, and then begin again, and find the other Sweep, that they would have the roundest: An *Example* of this will make it more plain, as in the following Figure will appear.

Let DE represent the length of a Rising-line EI, the height thereof 8 Foot on the after-end thereof: First, I find the Sweep that sweepeth it, by multiplying 20 Feet the length, which is 240 Inches: For if you look in the Tables under the Title of *Feet Inches*, for 20 Feet, you will see in the next Column toward the Left-hand, 240, over head is written *Inches*, signifying, that in 20 Feet is 240 Inches, and just against it, and in the same Line, towards the Right-hand, under the Title of *Squares*, you will see written 57600, signifying, that the Square of 240 is 57600, these Numbers you will find in the second Page of the Tables, and the fortieth Line, the fourth, fifth and sixth Columns.

F This

The Compleat Ship-Wright

This squared Number 57600, made by the Multiplication of *DE* 240 Inches must be divided by the height of the Rising-line assigned *E I* 8 Foot or 96 Inches, so remaineth in the Quotient 600, to which must be added the height of the Rising, as is afore taught, and they make 696 which is the Diameter of the whole Circle; the half thereof is 348 Inches, which is 29 Feet, as you may see by dividing it by 12; or else, if you turn to the Tables, and seek under the Title of *Inches* for 348, you will see in the same Line, toward the Left-hand, 29 Feet, which you will find in the third Page, and the forty-eighth Line, the first and second Column; then I work by that Sweep to ⅓ of the length of the Rising-line, or 12 Feet of the same; at the Point *C* it is represented, at which Point I seek the Rising *C B*, I seek in the Table for the *Square* made of 144, and I find in the first Page, forty-fourth Line, at the seventh Column, and towards the Right hand under the Title of *Squares*, I find 20736, which is the Square made of 144: Then I seek for the *Square* made of the Sweep, or the Side *A B*, 348 *Inches*, and I find it in the Tables to be 121104, from this 121104 I subtract the other *Square*, made of the Side *D C*, 144 being 20736, and there remaineth 100368, whose Root I find in the Tables, in the third Page, and the seventeenth Line, and the third Column, 100489, which is too much by near 121; but the other Number afore it being much more too little, the Number answering hereunto is 316 *Inches*, and near ¼, subtracted from 348, the whole side leaveth 31 Inches ¼, or 2 Foot 7 Inches ¼ for the Rising at the Point *C*: Now to make a rounder Sweep aftward, or at the other end of the Line, as from *B* to *P*, which runneth higher up, or roundeth more from *I* to *F*: Here will be something more of trouble to find the Sweep that will exactly touch the two Points assigned, as *B* and *F*. Now the way will be thus:

Let *B* and *F* be the two Points to which the Sweep is confined to touch; draw a strait Line from *B* to *F*, and so you have a right-angle Triangle made of the Sides *B H*, the length of the Line to be swept by the second Sweep; and the Side *H F*, the height of the same; together with the subtending Side *B F*: Then a Line drawn from the middle of the Side *B F*, perpendicular or square, to the same Line *B F*, and extended till it touch the Side *D A*; the place where it toucheth shall be the Center of the same Sweep: As is the Line

The Compleat SHIP-WRIGHT. 43

Line *G H*, paſſing through the middle of the Side *B F*, at the Point *O*. Which to find arithmetically, proceed thus: Find firſt the length of the Side *B F*, as is before taught, having two ſides of a right-angled Triangle given, to find the third ſide, which will be 134 ¼ Inches ; the half is 67 Inches ¼ from *B* to *O* ; then if a Perpendicular be let fall from *O* to the Line *B H*, it will cut that Baſe-line *B H* alſo in halves, in the Point *P*, making *B P* equal to *P H*, and each 48 Inches: Then again, the Side *O H* will be (in this Example) equal to the Side *B O*, but in other Caſes it may not ſo fall out: So then theſe two Sides being known, *O H*, 67 ½ Inches, and *P H* 48 Inches, with the Side *K H*, 240 Inches ; you may find *G H* by the *Rule of Three*, ſaying, if *P H* 48 give *O H* 67 ½ Inches, what will *K H* 240 Inches give.

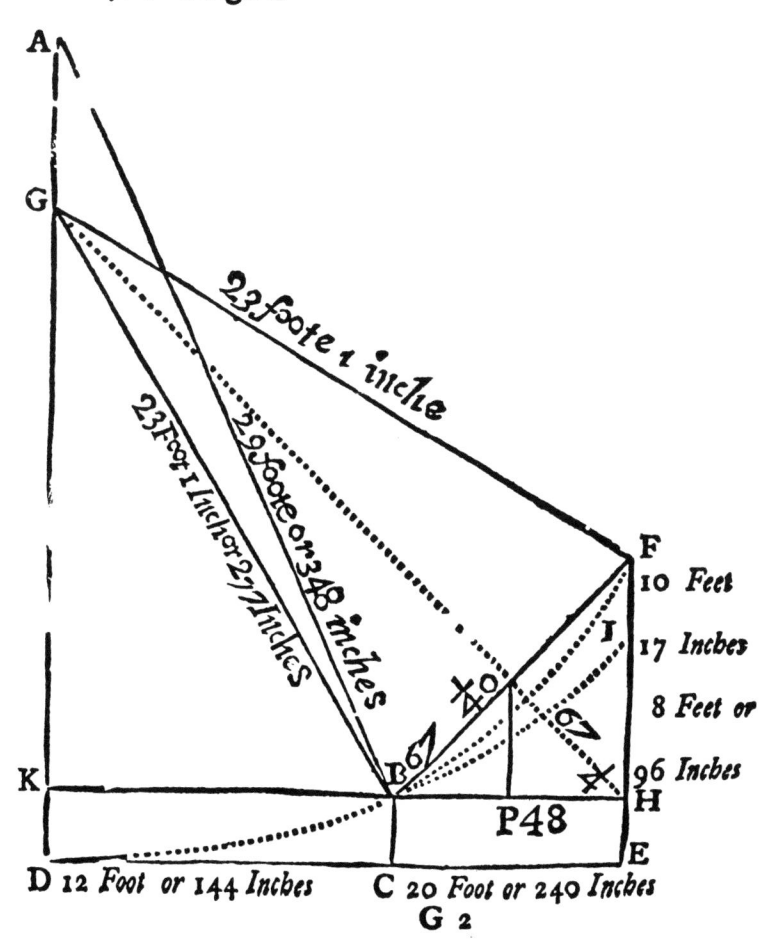

If 48 give 67 ½, what will 240?

```
        240            2
         67          144
       ----         4640
       1680        86080 (335
       1440         4988
       -----          44
      16080
```

If you multiply the two laſt Numbers together, and divide by the firſt Number, you will beget in the Quotient 335, for the Side *GH*.

I here neglected the ½ Inch in this Multiplication, for the ½ Inch ſhould have been multiplied into the 240, by adding to 16080, 120, the half of 240, and it maketh 16200, which divided by 48, maketh 337 ½ Inches for *GH*; ſo then theſe two ſides *KH* 240, and *GH* 337 ½ being found; find the Side *GK* thus, look in the Table of *Squares* for the *Square* made of *GH* 337, and it will be 113569, from which ſubtract the *Square* of *KH* 240, being 57600, there wreſteth 55969, that Number ſought for in the Tables, and the neareſt Number to it, is 56069, and the Root of it 237 is the ſide *GK*, to which add the Riſing *CB*, or *KD*, that is 31 ¼ Inches added to 237, maketh 268 ¼ Inches, or 22 Foot 4 Inches; ſhewing that at 22 Foot 4 Inches, from the Point *D*, towards *G*, will be the Point where the Center of the rounder Circle ought to ſtand: Then again, you have *GK* 237, and *KB* 144, to find *GB* being the longer ſide, you muſt add the Squares made of the other 2 ſides together, and the Square Root of thoſe 2 Sums ſhall be the longeſt ſide *GB*, that is, the Square of *GK* 237 is 56069, and the Square of *KB* 144 is 20736; theſe being added together is 76805, whoſe Square Root neareſt is 277 Inches or 23 Feet 1 Inch for *GB* the ſecond Sweep. The ſame order you may obſerve to round your Sweep, as often as you pleaſe.

```
113569
 57600
------
 55969
```

```
  237
  31 ¼
  ----
  268 ¼
```

```
 56069
 20736
------
 76805
```

Note, That when you ſeek for any Number in the Tables, take heed that you mind the Number of Figures you ſeek for, to agree in Number with thoſe that direct you to ſeek for them.

The Compleat SHIP-WRIGHT.

As for *Example*, in the other Figures above-mentioned, 55969, they are in Number 5, by their places, as you see; then repairing to the Table, I find 559504; but telling the Figures, I see they are in Number 6, but should be but 5: Therefore this Number, represented in the fifth Page, and the forty-eighth Line, and the last Column, is not the place I seek for, then I turn toward the beginning of the Table, till I see that the Columns of *Squares* contain but 5 Figures, and there seek the nearest Number agreeing to 55969; and in the second Page, thirty-seventh Line, sixth Column, I find 56069, the nearest agreeing to it, which is the place answering to the other directory Figures.

Note also, That the *Example* of finding the Sweep aforegoing, is laid down by a small Scale of the *Draught*, by which you may try it for your better Directions.

And in that Table you may see that any farther than 70 Foot, being the end of the fifth Column, sixth Page, I have not mentioned the *Feet* and *Inches* belonging to the Number of *Inches*, but have left it out because they are of little Use any farther; because that will reach far enough for the length of any Rising-line of any Ship whatever. If any be desirous to convert any of the following Numbers into Inches, he may do it by dividing by 12.

Thus, I think, I have spoken enough to the Ingenious, concerning the singular Use of the Tables, or of this way of working by Segments or Circles.

CHAP. XI

Concerning Measuring of Ships.

MUltiply the length of the Keel into the breadth of the Ship, at the broadest place, taken from out-side to out-side, and the Product of that by the half breadth, this second Product of the Multiplication divide by 94 for King's Tunnage, or 100 for Merchants Tunnage; and according to that Division, the Quotient thereof is so many Tuns: As suppose in the former *Draught*, being in length 60 Foot, and being multiplied by 20, the breadth produce 1200, and 1200 again multi-

$$\begin{array}{r} 60 \\ 20 \\ \hline 1200 \\ 10 \\ \hline 12000 \end{array}$$

plied

plied by 10, the half breadth produce 12000, if you divide by 100, you need do no more than cut off the two laſt Figures toward the Right-hand; which ſhall be the Anſwer, and rendreth the Ship to be 120 Tuns, but if you divide the Sum 12000 by 94, you wil have 127 $\frac{2}{3}$ of a Tun very near: But this cannot be the true Ability of the Ship to carry or lift, becauſe two Ships, by this Rule of equal Breadth and Length, ſhall be of equal Burden, notwithſtanding the fulneſs or ſharpneſs of thoſe Veſſels, which may differ them very much, or the one Ship may have more Timber than the other in her Building, and ſo ſhall carry leſs than the other: But the true way of Meaſure muſt be by Meaſure of the Body and Bulk of the Ship under Water; for if one Ship be longer in the Floor than another of the ſame breadth and length, ſhe ſhall be more in burden than the other; as a *Flemiſh* Ship ſhall carry more than a *French* or *Italian* Veſſel of the ſame length and breadth: Therefore, I ſay, the Meaſure of a Ship is known by meaſuring her, as a piece of Timber may be meaſured of the ſame form, to the draught of the Water aſſigned her, the weight of the ſame Body of the ſame Water that the Ship ſwimmeth in, ſhall be the exact Weight of the Ship, and all Things therein; Loading, Rigging, Victuals, included therein: Then if the Ship be meaſured to her light Mark as ſhe will ſwim at being lanched, the weight of ſo much Water being taken or ſubtracted from the weight of the Water when ſhe is laden, the Reſidue ſhall be the weight that muſt load her, or her Ability of carrying, called her Burden. By this Means you may know the Weight of the Ship light, and what ſhe will carry to every Foot of Water aſſigned her, which can be done by no general Rules in *Arithmetick*, becauſe of their greater Irregularity, according to the differing Forms of Ships; you may, if you pleaſe, firſt meaſure the Content of the Keel and Poſt, Stem and Rudder, of all that is without the Plank, and under the Water-line, and note it by it ſelf; then meaſure the Body of the Ship in the Midſhips, by multiplying of the depth of the Water-line, and the breadth; then you may find the content of the Want by the circular part of the Ship under Water, being narrowed downward, and ſubtract this from the whole content of the Body found by the depth of the Water-line and breadth of the Ship, and this ſhall be the ſolid content of that part of the Ship, I mean in ſolid foot Meaſure of 1728 Inches to the Foot: Then proceed to the fore-part or the after-part of the Ship, and to 3 or 4 Timbers more, find the mean breadth at the narrowing aloft at the Water-line, and allow at the Floor and the mean Depth, and meaſure that piece of the Ship; as I told you

you of the middle part of the Ship, and so measure the whole Ship by pieces, and add them together; and so many Feet as it maketh, so many Ifeet of Water shall be the Weight of the said Ship; and the Reason may be considered thus: There is a Ponderosity in the Water, but there is a greater in the Air; and there is a Ponderosity in the Water it self, but not so much as in other Things more solid, as in Iron; suppose a Gun, or an Anchor of Iron; it sinketh in the Water, but yet it is not so heavy in the Water as in the Air, by the weight of so much Water as shall make a Body not equal to the Body of the Gun, or an Anchor, in magnitude; which weight subtracted from the weight of the Iron Body weighed in the Air, and so much must be the Weight of it in the Water.

Again, If a Body be lighter in weight than Water of the same bigness, it hath an Ability of lifting in the Water, and can lift or carry so much as is that Difference: As a piece of Cork, or Wood of Fir-trees, being lighter than Water, it swimmeth on the face of the Water, and refuseth to be depressed without more weight added to it.

Thus a Ship being a concave Body, is made capable of lifting according to the greatness or littleness of this Concavity, respect being had to the greatness of the Timber put into it, or the Nature of it, all which maketh a Ship swim deeper or lighter in the Water.

I have proved by the *Thames* Water, that fresh Water is lighter than salt Water; so then salt Water being heavier than fresh, causeth that a Ship swimmeth deeper in the fresh Water than in salt.

But in the building of all Ships there is, or ought to be, a just Proportion used between the Length by the Keel, the Breadth by the Beam, and the Depth in the Hold, as also for the Rake fore and aft, &c. only with this Consideration as to what Use or Trade the Ship is intended for; some for Burden rather than Sailing, as Colliers, &c. and others chiefly for sailing, as Gallies and the like: But as gaging or measuring a Ship may properly be said to belong to Ships whose Burden is the chief thing enquired after, and as the Dimensions of all Ships as to length, breadth, depth in the Hold, rake fore and aft, &c. do not bear the same Proportion to one another, there ought, in the gaging or measuring, to be regard had to the depth in the Hold, as well as to the length and breadth; and therefore, both by Reason and my own Experience, I approve of the following Rule.

How

How to Gage a Ship.

It is certain, that if a Ship is gaged by only the length of the Keel, from the Heel to the Fore-foot, as the length of the Ship, all the Rake fore and aft is left; but to prevent this Error, Ships built for burden allow $\frac{3}{5}$ of the breadth for the Rake fore and aft, therefore the half of that, which is three tenths of the Breadth, added to the length of the Keel, or subtracted from the whole length of the Ship from Stem to Stern, reduces the Ship to very near a regular Solid, whose three Dimensions being multiplied together (as in other regular Solids) gives the solid Content, which divided by 39, the Quotient is the Tunnage of the Ship so measured.

To illustrate these Rules the better, I shall propose a Ship of the following Dimensions, being a Ship lately actually employed in the *Greenland* Trade.

	Feet	Inches
Length by the Keel	82	00
Whole Length, Rake and all	98	00
Consequently the Rake fore and aft	16	00
Breadth at the Beam	26	06
Depth in the Hold	12	00
Length by the Keel	82	00
Half Rake fore and aft add	8	00
Sum	90	00

Multiply the Breadth in Feet in Decimals— 26·5
By the Length ——— 90

Product ——— 2385
Multiply by the depth in Feet —— 12

Divide (always) by ——— 93) 28620 (307
                                720
                                ——
                                69

The Burden is 307 Tun and $\frac{6\cdot9}{9\cdot3}$ or $\frac{2\cdot3}{3\cdot1}$, or about three Quarters of a Tun.

The Compleat SHIP-WRIGHT.

As to the Tunnage of Colliers Ships, it is allowed that every Keel of Coals is 20 Tun, and therefore a Ship of 400 Tuns Burden will carry 20 Keels of Coals, (speaking of the Keels of *Newcastle*) and every Keel at *Newcastle* makes out 16 Chaldron at *London*. And as the Ships of Burden in the Coal Trade reckon by Scores of Chaldrons, a Ship of 400 Tun, or 20 Keels of Coals, makes out 16 Score (as the *Billingsgate* Phrase is) or 320 Chaldron of Coals.

It would seem that if we take first the solid Concavity of a Ship (if the Term may be allowed) and then take the Solidity of a Chaldron of Coals, both in Feet, Inches, or any other known Measure, the former divided by the latter, the Quotient would be the Chaldrons that that Ship would contain; and in this Case my Curiosity has led me to the following exact Calculation, both as to the Coal-bushel and the Coal-fatt, which is a quarter of a Chaldron; which Experiment I made aboard of a Collier when unloading in the Pool, and found the Dimensions of a Coal-Bushel and Fatt, and consequently the solid Content of a Chaldron of Coals as follows.

	Inches
Mean Diameter of the Coal Bushel	19 5
Height of the Cone or Heap above the top	7 7
Cubical Inches in the Heap	766 8
Cubical Inches in the Bushel within	2326 5
In all	3093 3
Multiply'd by 36, the Bushels in a Chaldron	36
Gives Inches in a Coal Chaldron	111359

Which Divided by 1728 is Cubical Feet 64, and 767 Inches.

But measuring also a Coal Fatt of which four makes a Chaldron, I found aboard of a Collier when unloading, as above, the Dimensions and Content of a Fatt of Coals as follows.

	Inches
Mean Diameter in Inches and Decimals	44 0
Depth	12 3
Height of the Heap	18 0
Content of the Conical Heap	9126 0
Content of the Fatt within	18710
In all	27836
Which multiplied by 4, the Fatts in a Chaldron	4

The Product is the Cubical Inches in a Chaldron of Coals, *viz.* — — 111344

Which divided by 1728, gives 64 Feet, and 752 Inches, differing but 15 Cubical Inches, from the former.

But this one thing is to be said, That altho' the Bushel and the Coal Fatt do so nearly agree, yet this Rule is not to be depended upon in large Ships; for where there is a great Bulk of Coals, as in a Ship of three or four Hundred Tun, the Weight of the uppermost presseth the undermost so close that, as far as I could estimate in a Ship of above twenty Keels of Coals, which makes about sixteen Score at *London*, the lowest Coals are so pressed by the uppermost, that a Chaldron, or 64 Foot, poured into the Ship, will not contain above 54 Foot, or little more, when so pressed together.

CHAP. XII.

Rules for MASTING *and* YARDING SHIPS *in Proportion to their Dimensions: And first, To find the Length of the Main-mast, which in a great measure governs all the rest, the Length by the Keel, the Breadth at the Beam, and the Depth in the Hold being known.*

FROM the length and breadth is gained the Main-masts length, and all the other Masts, also the Yards, are derived from thence, but there is different proceedings in this Case, according to the largeness

ness of the Ships; thus the Main-mast of small Ships are to be three times as long as the Ship is in breadth; as a Ship of 20 Foot broad, by the same Rule must have a Mast of 60 Foot long

Others for greater Ships add the breadth to the length, and to that the half breadth, which Sum they divide by five, and the Quotient is the number of Yards, as a Ship 114 Foot long and 34 Foot in breadth, the breadth added to the length, and the half breadth added thereto, make 165, that divided by 5, yields 33, and so many Yards is the length of that Mast; the Fore-mast must be a Yard shorter at the head. That is to say, besides the height of the Step, which in most Ships standeth higher from the bottom of the Ship than the Step of the Main-mast; the Fore-mast must be shorter by that difference, and one Yard more, the bigness of the Ship considered, may be 4 Foot shorter at the head, besides the difference below.

```
114
 34
 17
 ---
5) 165 (33
    15
    ---
     0
```

The Top-mast two thirds of the length of the lower Masts.

The Main-yard to be $\frac{2}{3}$ and $\frac{1}{12}$ of the Main-mast, as in the Mast aforementioned of 60 Foot long, $\frac{2}{3}$ of 60 is 40, and the $\frac{1}{12}$ of 60 is 5, added to 40 makes 45, for the length of the Main-yard.

The Fore-yard to be $\frac{6}{7}$ of the Main-yard, as the Main-yard being 45 Foot, divide 45 by 7, so cometh 6 in the Quotient, and a Fraction remaining of 3 signifying $\frac{3}{7}$, so that the $\frac{1}{7}$ of 45 will be 6 and $\frac{3}{7}$, you must take 6 times so much, as 6 times 6 makes 36, and if you take 6 times $\frac{3}{7}$, make $\frac{18}{7}$, that is two whole Numbers and $\frac{4}{7}$, which added to 36, make 38 and $\frac{4}{7}$ of a Foot for the length of the Fore-yard.

The Top-sail Yards must be half the length of the lower Yard, the Mizen-yard usually is made of equal length with the Fore-yard, the Cross-jack-yard of equal length with the Main-top-sail-yard, and the Mizen-top-sail-yard to be half the length of the Cross-jack-yard.

The Mizen-mast to be of the length of the Main-top-mast from the upper Decks, and so much longer as is the height of the Ship between Decks; the Bolt-spreet to be of length equal to the Fore-mast from the upper Deck of the Fore-castle upwards.

For the bigness of these Masts, to a Yard in length $\frac{1}{4}$ of an Inch, or else $\frac{1}{4}$ of an Inch to the Foot, and so of Yards likewise, only the Bolt-spreet something bigger, would be the better if it be made as big as the Fore-mast.

The Spreet-sail-yard in length ⅔ of the Bolt-spreet, the Sprit-sail-top-sail-yard as of the rest, to be ½ the Spreet-sail-yard, the Mizen-yard in bigness, but ½ Inch to a Yard: And directing my course to young Men that desire Instructions, I will avoid troubling of them as near as I can with Arithmetick, therefore I will shew them the sweeping out of Masts and Yards, for the filling up of their Quarters according to their Circles. Thus, make a half Circle equal in Diameter to the bigness of the Mast, in the Partners, for if it be a Topmast, equal to his bigness in the Cap; as suppose, for to make a Mast 60 Foot in length, then by the former Directions ¼ of an Inch for his bigness to a Foot, rendreth him to be 15 Inches thorough; but for a Main-mast, it is always better that they be made bigger, to every 6 Inches added ½ of an Inch more, so then this Mast will be 16 ¼ Inches, I make a sweep of 16 ¼ Inches, as from *A* to *B*, supposing the Feet

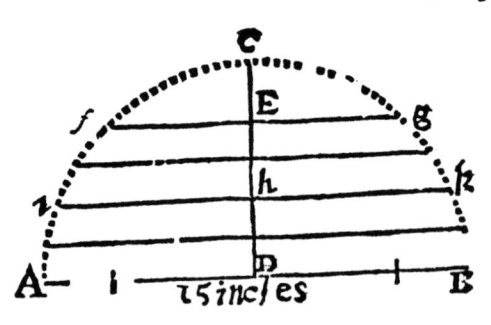

of the small Scale to be Inches, draw the Sweep or Arch *A C B*, 15 Inches from *A* to *B*, then at the Center draw a Line perpendicular to *A B*, as from *D* to *C*, divide the Perpendicular into four equal Parts with the Compasses, and set off three of them on the Perpendicular from *D* to *E*, and through that Point draw a Line parallel to *A B*, as is the Line *f g*, which shall be the bigness of the Mast at the Hounds, then middle the Space between *D* and *E*, as at *h*, and draw the Line *i k*, parallel to *A B*, which shall be the bigness of the Mast at the middle, then two other Lines drawn again through the middle between *D h* and another between *h E*, shall be the bigness of the Mast in the quarters, so then take off from the Sweep, the bigness at each place from the middle Line *D C*, to the Arch, and in like manner middle the Mast from the Partners to the Hounds, and quarter it, and strike a middle Line from end to end, and at each place set off the thickness found by your Sweep; for the length of the Heads of the Masts you

may

MASTING and YARDING.

may allow to every Foot 1 Inch ¼ of an Inch from the Head to the upper part of the Cross-trees; the length of the Trestle-trees to be ⅓ of the Ship's breadth, and in depth half the thickness of the Head at the Hounds, and for the thickness, half the thickness of the Head, at the end of the Head of the Mast: For Yards you may draw the Sweep of them to their bigness at the Slings, and let the ends of them be but one third of the bigness in the Slings, accordingly draw your Sweep and fill him out in the Quarters, according to the Circle, which I shall leave to your Practice.

But there are other Ways, which according to the Size of the Ship and the Trade she is intended for, not forgetting the Commander's Fancy, which will bear a great sway.

The first, which is the most rational Way, is to add the Breadth and Depth of the Ship together; and double it, and divide the Product by 3, and the Quotient is the Length of the Main-mast in Yards. *Example*, In the Ship we have propounded below, the Breadth 29 ½, the Depth 13 Foot, those two added is 42 ½, the double of 42 ½ is 85; that divided by 3, the Quotient is 28 ⅓ Yards, that is 85 Foot; but we have propounded our Mast to be but 84 Foot, and from this Foundation the following Table of Masts and Yards is proportioned

A Table of the Lengths and Thickness of the MASTS *and* YARDS *of a Ship that is* 75 *Foot by the Keel,* 29 ½ *Foot at the Beam, and* 13 *Foot in Hold, which is of the Burden of* 300 *Tun.*

	Length in Feet.	Thickness in Inches.
The Sprit-sail Top-sail-yard	14	4
The Fore-top-gallant-yard and the Spreet-sail Top-mast	16	5
The Main Top-gallant-yard	18	6
The Fore-top-gallant-mast	19	6
The Mizen-top-sail Yard	20	6
The Main Top-gallant-mast	21	7
The Mizen-top-mast	27	8
The Fore-top-sail-yard	31	9
The Main Top-sail-yard, 11 Inches, and Cross-jack-yard	36	7½
The Fore-top-mast	37	13
The Main Top-mast	42	14
The Sprit-sail-yard	50	16
The Mizen-mast	52	17
The Mizen-yard	51	16

Masting and Yarding.

	Length in Feet.	Thickness in Inches
The Fore-yard	62	20
The Bowsprit	66	22
The Main-yard	74	24
The Fore-mast	75	25
The Main-mast	84	28

A second Way is thus: Add the Length of the Keel, the Breadth of the Beam, and the Depth together, and to that Sum add the Difference between the Breadth and twice the Depth, and multiply the whole Sum by the Breadth at the Beam, and the Product divide by the former whole Sum, and the Quotient is the Length of the Main-mast in Yards. *Example,* In the Ship we have propounded the Length of the Keel to be 75 Foot, the Breadth of the Beam 29 ½ Foot, and the Depth 13 Foot, added together, the Sum is 117 ½, unto which add the Difference between twice the Depth 26, and the Breadth 29 ½, which divided by 121, the former whole Sum, the Quotient is 29 ¼ Yards, which is a Yard more than it was the other way; but it is too long, and therefore we commend the first way for the more rational way, and do persuade those that have occasion, to make use of that way.

Now having found the Length of the Main-mast in this manner, for any Ship, we have set down a Table of the Lengths and Thickness of all the Masts and Yards of the Ship we have propounded, by means whereof, after the Length and Thickness at the Partners of the Main-mast for any Ship is found, the Length and Thickness of all the other Masts and Yards may be found out by our Table, as followeth: Suppose a Ship 63 Foot by the Keel, 25 Foot at the Beam, and 11 Foot deep in Hold; we desire to know the Length and Thickness of all the Masts and Yards: And first for the Main-mast, the Breadth at Beam 25 Foot, the Depth 11 Foot, their Sum 36, their Double 72, which divide by 3, the Quotient is 24 Yards, the Length of the Main-mast, which is 72 Foot. To find the Lengths and Thickness of all the other, you may do it by the *Rule of Three,* the Lengths in Feet, and the Thickness in Inches, and the Proportion is from the Lengths and Thickness of the Masts and Yards, for they are but a lineal Proportion: That is,

As 84, the Length of our Main-mast in the *Table,* is to 72 the Length of the Main-mast found; so is 28 the Thickness of the Main-mast

maſt in the Table to 24, the Thickneſs of the Main-maſt found at the Partners: The Thickneſs of the Diameter at the Hounds muſt be $\frac{2}{3}$ of that which is at the Partners, which in this is 16 Inches Thickneſs or Diameter. Or this Proportion of the Length of the Maſts may be abbreviated, for it is as 7 to 6, ſo is 28 to 24; and ſo we proceed to find all the reſt, as 7 to 6, ſo is 75 our Fore-maſt to 64, the Length of the Fore-maſt required; and ſo we may proceed for all the other Lengths and Thickneſs, both of the Maſts and Yards: But

The Method uſed in Deptford-yard *is as follows:*

To find the Length of the Main-maſt, take half the Length of the Keel, and the Breadth of the Beam, and add them together and divide them together by 3, and that is your Length in Yards.

Your Fore-maſt muſt be $\frac{8}{9}$ of your Main maſt.

The Mizen-maſt muſt be $\frac{2}{3}$ of your Main-maſt, if it ſtands upon Deck, but if in the Hold, $\frac{3}{4}$ of your Main-maſt.

The Bowſprit muſt be $\frac{8}{9}$ of your Fore-maſt.

The Main Top-maſt, $\frac{1}{2}$ of your Main-maſt.

The Main Top-gallant-maſt, $\frac{1}{2}$ of your Main Top-maſt.

The Fore-top-maſt, $\frac{1}{2}$ of your Fore-maſt.

The Fore-top-gallant-maſt, $\frac{1}{2}$ of your Fore-top-maſt.

The Mizen-top-maſt, $\frac{1}{2}$ of your Mizen-maſt.

To find the Length of your Main-yard, take thrice the Breadth of your Beam, and a half, add them together and divide by 3; and that gives you the Length in Yards.

The Main Top-ſail-yard, $\frac{1}{2}$ your Main yard.

The Main-top-gallant-yard, $\frac{1}{2}$ of your Main Top-ſail-yard.

The Fore-top-ſail-yard, $\frac{1}{2}$ of your Fore-yard.

The Fore-top gallant-yard, $\frac{1}{2}$ of your Fore-top-ſail-yard.

The Croſs jack-yard, muſt be the Length of your Main Top-ſail-yard.

CHAP.

CHAP. XIII.
Of Rigging a SHIP.

Having thus given Directions, first, for *Building*; and secondly, for *Masting* and *Yarding a Ship*; the third Thing proposed is, to *Rigg her with Ropes* of a suitable Length and Size: And, first, for the Length of the Ropes of any Ship, the Length of whose Masts and Yards is given or found as before: Observe the following Rules.

It is observed by all that understand the Rigging of Ships, That all the Cordage that belongs to the Masts, shall hold in proportion according to the Length of the Masts above the first Deck. And for the Cordage that belongs to the Yards, if the Yards be longer or shorter than a Proportion given, first find the Length of the Cordage belonging to the Yards, according to the Proportion given; then as the Length of the Yard, according to the Proportion given, is to the Length of the Yard you would have your Cordage for; so is the Length of each particular Cordage found (according to the Proportion given) to the Length of the Cordage for the Yard you desire to have it.

For the Weight of Anchors and Cables, they are such Things as are Arbitrary, left to the Discretion of the Master, or other that hath to do in the Business, according as they find the Built of the Ship to be: And the like arbitrary it is in the Sizes of some of the Cordage and Ground Tackle. But first for the Length of the Ropes, the Length of the Masts and Yards being given.

A plain and easie Rule to Rigg any Ship by the Length of her Masts and Yards, without any further Trouble.

For the Sprit-sail-yard.
Halliards, three times the Length of the Yard.
Lifts, three times the Length of the Yard.
Clue-lines, two times the Length of the Yard.
Braces, two times the Length of the Fore-yard.
Bunt-lines, two times the Length of the Yard.
Sheets, three times the Length of the Yard.
Pennants, one third of the Yard.

Of Rigging a SHIP.

For the Sprit-fail Top-maft.

Shrouds, muft be the Length of the Maft from the Heel to the Crofs-trees.
Halliards, three times the Length of the Maft.
Lifts, three times the Length of the Maft.
Clulines, two times the Length of the Sprit fail-yard.
Braces, two times the Length of the Sprit-fail-yard.
Cranlines, two times the Length of the Top-fail-yard.

For the Fore-maft.

Pennants, $\frac{1}{3}$ of the Length of the Shrouds.
Shrouds, two thirds of the Maft.
Stay, one time the Length of the Maft wanting one fixth.
Lifts, three times the Length of the Shrouds.
Clugarnets, three times the Length of the Shrouds.
Buntlines, two times the Length of the Maft from the Deck to the Crofs-trees.
Leechlines, two times the Length of the Main-yard.
Braces, two times the Length of the Main-yard.
Forefheets, two and $\frac{1}{2}$ times the Length of the Main-yard.
Jeers, four times the Length of the Maft from the Deck to the Crofs-trees.
Buntlines, two times the Length of the Main-yard.
Topfail-fheets, two times the Length of the Main-yard.

The Fore-top-maft Rigging.

Pennants, one third of the Shrouds.
Shrouds, one time the Length of the Maft from the Crofs-trees to the Feed-hole.
Burtons, one time the Length of the Fore-yard.
Lifts, two and $\frac{1}{2}$ times the Length of the Fore-yard.
Clulines, three times the Length of the Fore-yard.
Braces, two and one third times the Length of the Fore-yard.
Bowlines, two and $\frac{1}{2}$ times the Length of the Fore-yard.
Leechlines, two times the Length of the Fore-top-fail-yard.
Tye, one time the Length of the Top-maft.
Runner, one and one third time the Length of the Fore-yard.
Halliards, three times the Length of the Fore-yard.
Stay, one and one third times the Length of the Maft.
Back-ftays, one and one third times the Length of the Fore-yard.
Buntlines, two times the Length of the Fore-yard.

The Fore-top-gallant Rigging.

Shrouds, one time the Length of the Mast from the Cross-trees to the Feed-hole.
Stay, one and a half times the Length of the Fore-yard.
Lifts, three times the Length of the Mast.
Braces, two and a half times the Length of the Fore-yard.
Bowlines, two and a half times the Length of the Fore-yard.
Halliards, two and a half times the Length of the Fore-yard.

For the Main-mast Rigging.

Pennants, one third of the Shrouds.
Shrouds, two thirds of the Mast.
Stay, the Length of the Mast.
Jeers, four times the Length of the Mast from the Deck to the Cross-trees.
Lifts, three times the Length of the Main-yard.
Braces, two and half times the Length of the Main-yard.
Bowlines, one time the Length of the Main-yard.
Clugarnet, two and half times the Length of the Main-yard.
Buntlines, four times the Length of the Mast for Falls and Ledges.
Leechlines, two times the Length of the Main-yard.
Tacks, one time the Length of the Main-yard.
Runners, one time the Length of the Main-yard.
Tacklefalls, three times the Length of the Runners.
Sheets, two and half the Length of the Main-yard.
Eknaveline, two times the Length from the Cross-trees to the Deck.
Topsail-sheets, two times the Length of the Main-yard.

The Main-top-mast Rigging.

Pennants, one third of the Shrouds.
Shrouds, one time the Length of the Mast.
Stay, one and a half time the Length of the Mast.
Braces, two and one third the Length of the Yard.
Burtons, one third of the Main-yard.
Lifts, two and half of the Length of the Main-yard.
Buntlines, two times the Length of the Main-yard.
Clulines, three times the Length of the Main-yard.
Tye, one time the Length of the Top-mast Shroud.
Runners, one time the Length of the Main-yard.
Halliards, three times the Length of the Main-yard.
Leechline, two times the Length of the Top-sail-yard.
Buntlines, two times the Length from the Deck to the Hounds.

Top-rope,

Of Rigging a Ship.

Top-rope, one time the Length of the Main-shrouds.
Top-tackle-fall, two times the Length of the Main-mast.
Pennant, one third of the Top-sail-yard
For Braces.
Backstays, one and half the Length of the Main-yard.

The Main Top-gallant-mast Rigging.

Shrouds, once the Length of the Mast from the Cross-trees to the Heel.
Stay, one and half the Length of the Main-yard.
Lifts, three times the Length of the Top-gallant-mast.
Braces, two times the Length of the Main-yard.
Bowlines, two times the Length of the Main-yard.
Tye, the Length of the Mast.
Halliards, two and half times the Length of the Main-yard.
Top Rope, two times the Length of the Main-yard.

Rigging for the Mizen-mast.

Halliards, four times the Length of the Mast from the Deck to the Cross-trees.
Braytles, two times the Length of the Mast from the Deck to the Cross-trees.
Sheet, one time the Length of the Yard.
Tack, three Fathoms length.
Shrouds, one time the Length of the Mast from the Deck to the Cross-trees.
Pennants, one third of the Shroud.
Burtenfal, one time the Length of the Main-yard.
Stay, one time the Length of the Mast.
Bowlines, one time the Length of the Cross-jack-yard.

Rigging for the Mizen-top-mast.

Pennants, one third of the Shroud.
Shrouds, the Length of the Mast from Cross-trees to the Heel.
Stay, one and half the Length of the Mast.
Lifts, three times the Length of the Mast.
Braces, one and one third the Length of the Mizen-yard.
Bowlines, one and half the Length of the Cross-jack-yard.
Cross-jack-braces, two and half the Length of the Cross-jack-yard.
Sheets, two and half the Length of the Cross-jack-yard.
Clulines, two and half the Length of the Cross-jack-yard.
Halliards, one and half the Length of the Mizen-yard.
Tye, one time the Length of the Top-mast from the Cross-trees to the Heel.

A Table

A Table of the NAMES, *the* SIZES, *the* NUMRER, *and the* LENGTHS *of each Rope, of Rigging, belonging to the fore-propounded Ship.* See Page 53.

1. Cordage of 1 Inch 1/13 Parts.

		Fa.	Fa.
2 Fore-top-gallant Braces	—	25	50
4 Fore-top-gallant Bowline-bridles	— —	1	4
2 Fore-top gallant Lifts	— —	22	44
8 Main-top-gallant Lanniards	— —	1½	12
4 Main-top-gallant Bowline-bridles	— —	1	4
1 Main Flag-ftaff-ftay	— —	11	11
8 Mizen-top-maft Lanniards	—	1½	12
1 Fall of the Mizen-top-fail Cranlines	—	36	36
2 Mizen-top-fail Bowlines	— —	12½	25
2 Mizen-top-fail Braces	— — —	17	34

2. Cordage of 1 Inch 1/16 Parts.

8 Lanniards of Sprit-fail Top-maft	—	1⅓	12
2 Falls of the Sprit-fail Top-maft Tackles	—	6	12
1 Fall of the Sprit-fail Cranlines	—	18	18
1 Sprit-fail Top-fail Halliard	— —	6	6
2 Sprit-fail Top-fail Lifts	—	5	10
2 Pennants of the Sprit-fail Top-fail Braces	—	1	2
2 Sprit-fail Top-fail Braces	— —	10	20
2 Sprit-fail Top-fail Cluelines	— —	10	20
2 Fore-top-maft Tacklefalls —	—	13½	27
2 Falls of the Fore-top-gallant Back-ftays	—	18	36
1 Fore-top-gallant Halliard —	—	32	32
2 Pennants of Fore-top-gallant Braces	—	1½	3
2 Fore-top-gallant Bowlines	— —	24	48
2 Fore-top-gallant Cluelines —	—	22	44
6 Fore-top-gallant Lanniards —	—	1½	9
2 Falls of the Main-top-gallant Tackle	—	7	14
2 Falls of the Main-top-gallant Back-ftays	—	20	40
2 Main-top-gallant Lifts	— —	24	48
2 Main-top-gallant Braces	— —	28	56
2 Main-top-gallant Bowlines	— —	24	48
8 Mizen Brails	— —	8	64
2 Mizen-top-maft Tacklefalls	— —	9	18

1 Fall

Of Rigging a SHIP.

		Fa.	Fa.
1	Fall of the Mizen-top-fail Cranlines	36	36
6	Mizen-top-fail Bowline-bridles	1	6
2	Pennants of the Mizen-top-fail Braces	1	2
2	Crofs-jack Braces	20	40
2	Fore-top-fail Leechlines	10	20

3. Cordage of 1 Inch $\frac{8}{10}$ Parts.

2	Lanniards of the Sprit-fail ftanding Lifts	6	12
4	Fore Martlines Legs	22	22
2	Lanniards for the Hoffes for the Fore-yard	6	12
8	Lanniards for the Fore-top-maft Shrouds	2	16
2	Fore-top-fail Braces	$23\frac{1}{2}$	47
4	Fore-top-fail Bowline-bridles	2	8
2	Fore-top-gallant Parrel-ropes	1	2
10	Lanniards of the Main-top-maft Shrouds	$2\frac{1}{2}$	25
2	Main-top-fail Braces	24	48
2	Main-top-fail Leechlines	12	24
2	Main-top-gallant Cluelines	25	50
2	Pennants of the Main-top-gallant Braces	1	2
10	Lanniards for the Mizen Shrouds	$2\frac{1}{2}$	25
2	Pennants of the Crofs-jack Braces	3	6
1	Sling for the Crofs-jack-yard	3	3
2	Pennants of the Mizen-top-fail Cranlines	2	4
1	Mizen-top-fail Halliard, in three Parts	28	28
2	Mizen-top-fail Cluelines	14	28

4. Cordage of 2 Inches $\frac{8}{10}$ Parts.

2	Sprit-fail Braces	16	32
2	Sprit-fail Clueline	11	22
1	Sprit-fail Buntline, in 2 Parts	21	21
8	Sprit-fail Top-maft Shrouds	3	24
2	Pennants of the Sprit-fail Top-fail Tackles	2	4
3	Pennants of the Sprit-fail Top-fail Cranlines	8	8
10	Puttocks of the Sprit-fail Top-maft Shrouds	10	10
2	Sprit-fail Top-maft Parrel-ropes	2	2
2	Fore-fail Martlines-falls	29	58
5	Fore-fail Buntlines	16	80
2	Fore-braces	15	30
2	Fore-top-fail Lifts	18	36
		2 Falls	

Of Rigging a Ship.

		Fa.	Ft.
2	Falls of the Fore-top-maſt Back-ſtay	4½	9
2	Pennants of the Fore-top-ſail Braces	3	6
1	Lanniard of the Fore-top-maſt's Stay	5	5
2	Fore-top-ſail Bowlines	26	52
2	Fore-top-ſail Buntlines	10	20
2	Pennants of the Fore-top-gallant Back-ſtay	4	4
1	Fore-top-gallant Tye	3½	3½
8	Fore-top-gallant Puttocks	8	8
1	Fore-top-gallant Stay	18	18
1	Fore-top-gallant Top-rope	27	27
6	Fore-top-gallant Shrouds	3½	21
4	Main ſail Martlines Legs	8	32
2	Falls of the Main-top-maſt Tackles	15½	31
2	Lanniards of the Main-top-maſt Back-ſtays	5	10
2	Main-top-ſail Lifts	24½	49
2	Main-top-ſail Buntlines Falls	17½	35
2	Main-top-ſail Buntlines Legs	9½	19
2	Pennants of the Main top-gallant Tackles	2½	2½
2	Pennants of the Main-top-gallant Back-ſtays	4	4
1	Main-top-gallant Halliard	37	37
10	Main-top-gallant Puttocks	13	13
2	Main-top-gallant Parrel-ropes	1	2
2	Falls of the Mizen Tackles	16	32
1	Mizen Truſs	12	12
1	Mizen Bowline	5	5
2	Pennants of the Mizen-top-maſt Tackles	1	2
8	Mizen-top-maſt Shrouds	4½	36
1	Mizen-top-maſt Tye	4½	4½
10	Puttocks of the Mizen-top-maſt Shrouds	1½	15
2	Mizen-top-maſt Parrel-ropes	1	2

5. Cordage of 2 Inches 1/8 Parts.

		Fa.	Ft.
1	Sprit-ſail Top-maſt Tye	3	3
2	Main-ſail Martlines Falls	32	64
2	Main Braces	24	48
8	Main-top-gallant Shrouds	4	32
2	Sprit-ſail Garnets	18	36
2	Sprit-ſail Lifts	18	36
2	Pennants of the Sprit-ſail Braces	1	2

Of Rigging a Ship. 63

		Fa.	Fa.
2	Sprit-fail Sheets	17	34
1	Hofs for the Stay	6	6
2	Fore-top-fail Cluegarnets	15	30
2	Fore-fail Bowline-bridles	4	4
2	Pennants of the Fore-braces	2	4
1	Lanniard of the Fore-top-maft Stay	4	4
2	Falls of the Fore-top-maft running Back-ftays	17	34
2	Fore-top-maft Parrel-ropes	3	3
1	Fore-top-maft Breft-rope	2	2
6	Main-fail Buntlines	9	54
1	Main Luff Tackle	8	8
1	Fall of the Main-fail Buntlines	54	54
1	Main Bowline Tackle	8	8
2	Lanniards of the Main-yard Hoffes	6	12
2	Falls of the Main top-maft running Back-ftays	$19\frac{1}{2}$	39
2	Main-top-maft Parrel-ropes	4	4
1	Main-top-gallant Maft-ftay	14	14
1	Main-top gallant Top-rope	30	30
1	Mizen Tack	2	2
2	Crofs-jack Lifts	15	30
1	Mizen-top-maft Top-rope	13	13
16	Lanniards of the Fore-fhrouds	4	64
2	Fore-top-fail Cluelines	30	60

6. Cordage of 3 Inches $\frac{1}{16}$ Parts.

1	Sprit-fail Halliard	17	17
2	Hoffes for the Sprit-fail Sheets	$1\frac{1}{2}$	3
2	Falls of the Boats-Tackles for the Fore-maft	32	64
2	Other Falls	22	44
2	Fore-lifts	20	40
2	Fore-bowlines	15	30
2	Pennants of the Fore-top-maft Tackles	2	4
2	Pennants of the Fore-top-maft running Back-ftays	3	6
8	Fore-top-maft Shrouds	$6\frac{1}{2}$	52
10	Fore-top-maft Puttocks	$2\frac{1}{2}$	25
1	Fore-top-maft Halliards	35	35
2	Falls of the Boats Tackles for the Main-maft	35	70
2	Other Falls	23	46
2	Main Lifts	24	48

2 Main

Of Rigging a SHIP.

		Fa.	Fa.
2	Main Clue-garnets	18	36
2	Pennants of the Main Braces	2	4
1	Lanniard of the Main-top-maſt Stay	5	5
1	Main-top-ſail Halliard	44	44
2	Pennants of the Main-top-ſail Braces	1½	3
2	Main-top-ſail Bowlines	27	54
6	Main-top-ſail Bowline-bridles	2	12
2	Main-top-ſail Cluelines	35	70
1	Main-top-gallant Tye	4	4
2	Runners of the Mizen Tackles	8	16
1	Mizen Halliard	19	19
1	Mizen Sheet	13	13

7. Cordage of 3 Inches 1/8 Parts.

		Fa.	Fa.
2	Sprit-ſail Standing-lifts	7	14
1	Fore-top-maſt Stay	12½	12½
2	Fore-top-maſt ſtanding Back-ſtays	15½	31
1	Runner of the Fore-top-ſail Halliards	12	12
20	Lanniards of the Main-ſhrouds	4	80
2	Main Bowlines	17	34
4	Main Bowline-bridles	3	12
1	Main Garnet-fall	29	29
2	Pennants of the Main Tackles	2	4
10	Main-top-maſt-ſhrouds	7	70
2	Pennants of the Main-top-maſt Back-ſtays	7	14
2	Main-top-maſt ſtanding Back-ſtays	18	36
2	Pennants of the Main-top-ſail Braces	2	4
1	Main-top-maſt Breaſt-rope	2½	2½
2	Pennants of the Mizen Tackles	2	4
1	Mizen Jeer	12	12
1	Mizen Parrel-rope	3	3

8. Cordage of 3 Inches 1/3 Parts.

		Fa.	Fa.
1	Lanniard of the Fore-ſtay	5	5
10	Mizen Shrouds	8	80

9. Corda

Of Rigging a Ship.

9. *Cordage of 4 Inches* $\frac{4}{10}$ *Parts.*

		Fa.	Fa.
1	Fore-Halliards	30	30
3	Fore Parrel-ropes	8	8
1	Luff Hook-rope	7	7
2	Hoffes for the Fore-yard	6	6
1	Fall of the Fore-top-maft Top-rope	18	18
1	Main Garnet-guy	8	8
3	Main-parrel ropes	9	9
2	Hoffes for the Main-yard	8	8
1	Runner for the Main-top-fail Halliards	14	14
1	Fall of the Main-top Rope	21	21
10	Main-top-maft Puttock	3	30
1	Mizen-ftay	9	9

10. *Cordage of 4 Inches* $\frac{8}{10}$ *Parts.*

2	Pennants of the Sprit-fail-fheets	4	8
2	Fore-maft Runners of the Boats Tackles	13	26
2	Other Runners	12½	25
2	Fore-fheets	25	50
1	Fore-top-maft Tye	6¼	6¼
2	Main-maft Runners of the Boats Tackles	14	28
2	Other Runners	13	26
1	Main-top-maft Stay	12½	12½

11. *Cordage of 5 Inches* $\frac{1}{10}$ *Parts.*

2	Fore-top-fail Sheets	21	42
1	Lanniard of the Main-ftay	8	8
1	Main Halliard	40	40
2	Main Jeers	25	50
2	Main-fheets	30	60
1	Pennant of the Main-garnet	5	5
1	Main-top-maft Tye	8	8
1	Mizen Tye	7	7

12. *Cordage of 5 Inches* $\frac{5}{10}$ *Parts.*

1	Sling of the Sprit-fail-yard	2	2
4	Pennants of the Fore-tackles	3½	14
16	Fore-fhrouds	10	160
1	Fore Breaft-rope	2	2
			1 Collar

		Fa.	Fa.
1	Collar of the Fore-stay about the Bowsprit	3	3
1	Main Breast-rope	3	3
2	Main-top-sail Sheets	24	48

13. *Cordage of* 6 *Inches* $\frac{1}{18}$ *Parts.*

8	Wouldings for the Bowsprit	5	40
1	Fore Tye	14	14
2	Fore Tacks	12½	25
4	Pennants of the Main-tackle	4	16
20	Main-shrouds	11	220
1	Pennant of the Main-top-mast Top-rope	6	6

14. *Cordage of* 6 *Inches* $\frac{1}{18}$ *Parts.*

1	Main Tye	13	13
2	Main Tacks	15	30

15. *Cordage of* 10 *Inches* $\frac{1}{18}$ *Parts.*

1	Fore-stay	12	12
1	Collar about the Stem	5	5
1	Pennant of the Main-winding Tackle	6	6

16. *Cordage of* 14 *Inches.*

1	Main-stay	16	16

Of Rigging a Ship.

A Table *of the Thickness of all* Ropes *belonging to any* Ship, *from a Mast of* 12 *Inches to* 34 *Inches through.*

The USE *of the* TABLE.

FInd the Diameter of the Main-mast at the Top of the *Column*, and under that, and against the *Name of the Rope*, you have the *Thickness* of the said Rope.

EXAMPLE:

Suppose in a Ship whose Main-mast is 30 Inches through, and I desire to know the *Thickness* of the Main-stay: I look for the *Mast of 30 Inch.* at the top of the Table, *Page* 68, and under it, against [Stay] I find 15; which shews, that a Ship whose Main-mast is 30 Inches through, or in Diameter, requires a Main-stay of 15 Inches.

Again: If the Fore-top-gallant Stay of the same Ship is required, look in *Page* 74, for *The Bigness of Fore-top-gallant Rigging*; you will, under 30, the Diameter of the Main-mast, find 2 Inches the *Thickness* of the Fore-top-gallant Stay. And so in all others.

The Bigness of the Rigging for these Main-masts, and Main-top-masts. The Fore-mast to these Masts followeth in the next Page.	Mast of 34 Inch.	Mast of 32 Inch.	Mast of 30 Inch.	Mast of 29 Inch.	Mast of 28 Inch.	Mast of 27 Inch.	Mast of 26 Inch.	Mast of 24 Inch.	Mast of 23 Inch.	Mast of 19 Inch.	Mast of 13 Inch.	Mast of 12 Inch.
	1 Inch	2 Inch	3 Inch	4 Inch	5 Inch	6 Inch	7 Inch	8 Inch	9 Inch	10 Inch	11 Inch	12 Inch
Pennant of Tackles	8½	8	7	6½	6	5½	5	7	6	5	4	4
Runners	6	5½	5	5	4½	4	3½	5	5	4½	3½	3½
Falls of the Tackles	4	4	3½	3½	3	3	3	3½	3½	2½	2½	
Shrouds	8½	8	7½	7	6½	5	5	7	6	5	4	4
Lanniards	4½	4	4	3½	3	3	3	4	3½	3¼	2½	2½
Swifters	8½	8	7½	7	6½	5	5	5½	5	4½	3½	
Lanniards	4½	4	4	3½	3½	3	2½	3½	3	3	2½	
Stay	17	16	15	14½	14	10	8	12	11½	9½	6½	6
Collar at the Stem	16	15	13	12	11	9	8	10	10	8	6	
Lanniard of the Stay	6	5½	5½	5	4	4	3½	4	4	3½	2½	3
Lifts	4½	4	3½	3½	3	3	2½	3	3	2½	2½	2
Tacks	9½	9	8½	8	6½	6	5	6½	6	5½	4	4
Sheets	6½	6½	6	6	5	4½	4	4½	4½	3½	2½	3
Bowlines	5½	5	4½	4½	4	4	3	3	3	2½	2½	} 2½
Bridles	4½	4½	4	4	3½	3½	3	3	3	2½	2	
Pennants Fore-braces	4	4	3¼	3½	3	3	2¾	3	3	2½	2	2½
Braces	3	3	3	3	2½	2½	2	2½	2½	2	1½	2
Clue-garnets	4	3½	3	3	2½	2½	2	3	2½	2½	1½	2
Jeers	8½	8	7	6	5½	5		6	4½	4		
Parrel-rope	6	6	5	5	4½	4	3	4½	4	3½	3	3
Breast-rope	8	7	6	6	5							
Runner of Martlines	2½	2½	2½	2½	2	2						
Fall of Martlines	3	2¼	2¼	2	2	2		2½	2	2	1½	
Pennant of the Garnet	8½	8	7½	7	6	5	4½	6	5½	5	5	4
Tye	6	5½	5	5	4½	4	3½	3½	3½	3	3	3
Fall of the Garnet	4½	4	4	4	3½	3½	3	3	3	2¼	2	2
Main-top-mast Rigging	1	2	3	4	5	6	7	8	9	10	11	12
Pennant of Tackles	5	5	4½	4	3½	3	2¼	3½	3½	2½		2
Falls of Tackles	2½	2½	2½	2½	2	2	1½	2	2	1½		1½
Shrouds	5	5	4¼	4	4	3	3	4	3½	3	2¼	2½
Lanniards	2½	2½	2¼	2	2	2	1½	2	2	1½	1	1
Back-stays	5	5	5	4	3½	3	2½	4	4	3½	2	2½
Lanniards	3	3	3	2½	2½	2	2	2½	2	1½	1	1
Stay	8	7	6	5	5	4½	4	5	4½	3½	3	2½
Lanniard	4	4	3½	3½	3	3	2¼	3	2½	2	1½	2
Lifts	3½	3	2½	2½	2	2	2¼	2	2	1½	1	1

Note, *Their* Buntlines *are in Bigness as followeth,*

3½	3½	3	2½
2	2	2	2
2	2	2	1½

Note, *The Ships that have no* Jeers, *their* Tye *is* 4 Inches, *and their* Halliards *is* 2½.

T

The Bigness of Fore Rigging	1	2	3	4	5	6	7	8	9	10	11	12
Pennants of Tackles	8	7½	7	6	5	5	5	6¼	5½	4½	3½	6
Runners of Tackles	5½	5	5	5	4	4	4	5	5	4½	3	2½
The Falls	4	3½	3½	3½	3	3	3	3½	3	2½	2	
Shrouds	8	7½	6½	6	5½	5	4½	6	5½	4½	3½	3½
Lanniards	4	4	4	4	3½	2½	2	3½	3½	3	2	2
Swifters	8	7½	7	6	5½	5	4½					
Lanniards	4	4	4	4	3½	3½	3					
Stay	15	13	12	11	9	7	6½	10½	8½	7½	5	4
Lanniard	5	5	5	4½	4	3½	3	4	3½	3	2	2
Tye	8	7½	7	7	6	6	5	5½	5	5	3½	4
Halliards	6	6	6	5	4½	3½	3	3	3½	3	2	2
Jeers	6½	6	6	6	4	4	5½					
Lifts	4	3½	3½	3	3	2½	2	3	3	2½		2
Parrel-ropes	5	5	4½	4½	4	4	3	3	3	2½	2	2½
Breast-ropes	8	7	6½	6	5							
Sheets	6	6	5	5	4½	4	3½	4½	4	3½	2½	2½
Jacks	8½	8	7	7	6	5	4½	6	6	5	5	3½
Bowlines	4½	4½	4	3½	3½	3	3	3¼	3	2½	2	2½
Bridles	4½	4	3½	3	3	3	2	3½	3	2½	2	2
Pennants of Braces	4	3½	3	3	2½	2½	2½	3	3	2½	1½	2
Braces	3	3	2½	2½	2	2	2	2½	2½	2	1¼	1½
Clue-garnets	3½	3	3	2½	2	2	2	3	2½	2	1½	1½
Buntlines	3	3	2½	2½	2	2	2	2	2	2	1½	1½
Martline Runners	3	2½	2½	2½	2							
Martlines	2½	2½	2½	2½	2	2½	2	2	1½			

The Bigness of the Fore-top-sail Rigging.	1	2	3	4	5	6	7	8	9	10	11	12
Pennant of Tackles	4½	4	3½	3	2½	2½	3½	3½	3	2½		
Falls to them	2½	2	2	2	1½	1½	2	2	2	1½		
Shrouds	4½	4	3½	3½	3	3	2½	4	3	3	2	2
Lanniards	2	2	2	2	1½	1½	2	2	1½	1½	1	1
Puttocks	5	4½	4½	4	3½	3	2¼	3	3	2½	1½	
Stay	5	5	5	4½	4	3	3	4½	4	3½	2	2½
Pennant of the Lanniard	4	3½	3½	3	2½	2½	1¾					1½
Fall of the Lanniard	3½	3½	3	2½	2	2	2	3	2½	2	1½	1½
Tye	7	7	6½	6½	5½	5	5	6	5	3½	2	
Runner	5	5	4¼	4¼	4	4	4	4½	4	3½		
Halliards	5	4½	4	4	3½	3½	2¼	3	2½	2	1½	
Bowlines	4	3½	3	3	2½	2½	2½	2	2	1½	1¼	
Bridles	3½	3½	3	3	2½	2	1½	2	1½	1½	1½	
Cluelines	4¼	4	4	3½	3	2½	2	3	2½	1½	1½	
Parrel-rope	4	4	4	3¾	3½	3	2	3½	3	2½	2	

Of Rigging a Ship.

The Bigness of the Boltsprit Rigging.	Mast of 34 Inch.	Mast of 32 Inch.	Mast of 30 Inch.	Mast of 29 Inch.	Mast of 28 Inch.	Mast of 27 Inch.	Mast of 26 Inch.	Mast of 24 Inch.	Mast of 23 Inch.	Mast of 19 Inch.	Mast of 13 Inch.	Mast of 12 Inch.
	1 Inch	2 Inch	3 Inch	4 Inch	5 Inch	6 Inch	7 Inch	8 Inch	9 Inch	10 Inch	11 Inch	12 Inch
Pennants of Sheets	6	6	$5\frac{1}{2}$	$5\frac{1}{2}$	$4\frac{1}{2}$	4	$3\frac{1}{2}$	5	$4\frac{1}{2}$	4	3	$2\frac{1}{2}$
Sheets	$4\frac{1}{2}$	$4\frac{1}{2}$	4	3	3	$2\frac{1}{2}$	$2\frac{1}{2}$	4	$3\frac{1}{2}$	$3\frac{1}{4}$	3	$1\frac{1}{2}$
Cluelines	3	3	3	$2\frac{1}{2}$	2	2	2	3	$2\frac{1}{2}$	2	$1\frac{1}{2}$	$1\frac{1}{2}$
Garnets	$3\frac{1}{2}$	3	3	3	$2\frac{1}{2}$	$2\frac{1}{2}$	2	3	3	$2\frac{1}{2}$	$1\frac{1}{4}$	1
Pennants of Braces	4	4	3	3	$2\frac{1}{2}$	$2\frac{1}{2}$	$2\frac{1}{2}$	3	$2\frac{1}{2}$	2	$1\frac{1}{4}$	$1\frac{1}{2}$
Braces	$2\frac{1}{2}$	$2\frac{1}{2}$	$2\frac{1}{2}$	$2\frac{1}{2}$	2	2	2	$2\frac{1}{2}$	2	$1\frac{1}{4}$	$1\frac{1}{4}$	$1\frac{1}{2}$
Halliards	$4\frac{1}{2}$	4	$3\frac{1}{2}$	$3\frac{1}{2}$	$3\frac{1}{4}$	3	$2\frac{1}{4}$	$3\frac{1}{2}$	3	$2\frac{1}{4}$	$2\frac{1}{2}$	2
Tye	7	6	6	6	5	$4\frac{1}{2}$	4	6	5	5	$4\frac{1}{2}$	2
Buntlines	3	3	$2\frac{1}{2}$	$2\frac{1}{2}$	2	2	$1\frac{1}{2}$	$2\frac{1}{2}$	$2\frac{1}{2}$	2	$1\frac{1}{2}$	
Hosse	6	6	$5\frac{1}{2}$	$5\frac{1}{4}$	5	4	3	3	3	3	$2\frac{1}{2}$	$2\frac{1}{2}$
Lifts	4	3	3	3	$2\frac{1}{2}$	2	2	3	3	$2\frac{1}{2}$	2	$1\frac{1}{2}$

The Bigness of the Spritsail-top Rigging.	1	2	3	4	5	6	7	8	9	10	11	12
Shrouds	3	3	$2\frac{1}{2}$	$2\frac{1}{4}$	2	2	$1\frac{1}{2}$	$2\frac{1}{2}$	$2\frac{1}{4}$	2	$1\frac{1}{4}$	1
Lanniards	2	$1\frac{1}{4}$	$1\frac{1}{4}$	$1\frac{1}{2}$	1	1	1	2	$1\frac{1}{2}$	1	1	
Pennants of Braces	$2\frac{1}{2}$	$2\frac{1}{2}$	2	2	$1\frac{1}{2}$	$1\frac{1}{2}$	$1\frac{1}{2}$	2	$1\frac{1}{4}$	$1\frac{1}{2}$	$1\frac{1}{2}$	
Braces	2	$1\frac{1}{2}$	$1\frac{1}{2}$	$1\frac{1}{2}$	$1\frac{1}{2}$	1	1	$2\frac{1}{2}$	1	1	1	
Tye	3	3	3	$2\frac{1}{2}$	2	2	$1\frac{1}{2}$	1	$1\frac{1}{2}$	$1\frac{1}{2}$	$1\frac{1}{4}$	
Halliards	2	2	2	2	$1\frac{1}{2}$	$1\frac{1}{2}$	$1\frac{1}{2}$	2	$1\frac{1}{2}$	$1\frac{1}{4}$	1	1
Cluelines	$2\frac{1}{2}$	2	2	2	$1\frac{1}{2}$	$1\frac{1}{2}$	1	2	$1\frac{1}{2}$	$1\frac{1}{2}$	1	1
Pennants of Tackles	3	3	$2\frac{1}{4}$	2	$1\frac{1}{2}$	$1\frac{1}{2}$	$1\frac{1}{4}$	$1\frac{1}{2}$			$\frac{1}{4}$	
Falls to them	2	2	$1\frac{1}{4}$	$1\frac{1}{2}$	1	1	1					
Lifts	2	2	$1\frac{1}{2}$	$1\frac{1}{2}$	$1\frac{1}{2}$	$1\frac{1}{2}$	1	$1\frac{1}{4}$	$1\frac{1}{2}$	1	1	1
Puttocks	3	3	$2\frac{1}{2}$	2	2	2	2	$2\frac{1}{2}$	2	2	2	
Parrel-ropes	2	2	$1\frac{1}{4}$	$1\frac{1}{2}$	$1\frac{1}{2}$	$1\frac{1}{2}$	1	$1\frac{1}{4}$	$1\frac{1}{2}$	$1\frac{1}{2}$	1	1

Of Rigging a SHIP.

The Bigness of Mizen Rigging.

The Mizen-mast.	Mast of 34 Inch.	Mast of 32 Inch.	Mast of 30 Inch.	Mast of 29 Inch.	Mast of 28 Inch.	Mast of 27 Inch.	Mast of 26 Inch.	Mast of 24 Inch.	Mast of 23 Inch.	Mast of 19 Inch.	Mast of 13 Inch.	Mast of 12 Inch.
	1 Inch	2 Inch	3 Inch	4 Inch	5 Inch	6 Inch	7 Inch	8 Inch	9 Inch	10 Inch	11 Inch	12 Inch
Pennants of Tackles	5½	5	4½	4								
Runners	4	3½	3½	3								
Falls of Tackles	3	3	2½	2½								
Shrouds	5½	5	4¼	4½	3½	3	2½	4	4	3	2	2½
Lanniards	3	2½	2½	2½	2	2	1½	2	2	1½	1½	1½
Tye	7	6½	6	5	5	4½	4					
Halliards	5	4½	3½	3	2½	2½	2	3½	3	2½	2	
Stay	6	5	4	3½	3½	3½	3	4	4	3	2½	2½
Lanniards	3½	3	2½	2½	2	2	1½	2½	2	1½	1	1½
Sheet	4	3½	3	2½	2½	2½	2	3	3	2½	2	1½
Jeer	5½	5	4	3½	3½							
Truss	3½	3	2½	2½	2	2	1½	2½	2	2	1½	
Bowlines	4	3	2	2	2	2	1¼	2½	2	1½	1½	1½
Brayles	2½	2	2	2	2	2	1½	2	1¼	1½	1½	1
Parrel-rope	5½	5	4	3	3	3	2½	3½	3	2½	2	2

The Cross-jack.	1	2	3	4	5	6	7	8	9	10	11	12
Lifts	4	3½	2½	2½	2	1½	1	2½	2½	2	1½	1
Braces	2½	2½	2	2	1½	1	1	2	1¼	1½	1	1
Pennants	3½	3	2½	2¼	2	1½	1¼	2	1½	1¼	1	1
Halliards	4	3½	3	3	2½	2	1½	2	1¼	1½	1½	1½

Big-

Of Rigging a Ship.

Bigness of Mizen-top-mast Rigging.	Mast of 34 Inch.	Mast of 32 Inch.	Mast of 30 Inch.	Mast of 29 Inch.	Mast of 28 Inch.	Mast of 27 Inch.	Mast of 26 Inch.	Mast of 24 Inch.	Mast of 23 Inch.	Mast of 19 Inch.	Mast of 13 Inch.	Mast of 12 Inch.
	1 Inch	2 Inch	3 Inch	4 Inch	5 Inch	6 Inch	7 Inch	8 Inch	9 Inch	10 Inch	11 Inch	12 Inch
Pennants of Tackles	3½	3	2½	2½								
Falls of Tackles	2½	2¼	2	2								
Shrouds	3	3	2½	2½	2	1½	1	2	2			
Lanniards	2	1½	1½	1½	1½	1	1½	1	1¼			
Puttocks	3½	3	2½	2½	2	1½	2	1½	1½	1		
Pennants of Braces	2½	2½	2	1½	1½	1½	1	2	1½	1¼		
Braces	2	2	1¼	1½	1	1	1	1	1¼			
Bowlines	2½	2	1¼	1½	1¼	1	1	1½	1	¼		
Bridles	2	2	1½	1¼	1	1	1	1	1¼			
Cluelines	2	2	1¼	1½	1½	1½	1	2	1½	1½	1	1
Tye	3	3	3	2½	2½	2½	2	3	2	2	2	1½
Halliards	2½	2½	2	2	1½	1½	1¼	2	1½	1½	1½	1
Lifts	2	2	1¼	1½	1½	1½	1	1	1	1	¼	1
Parrel-rope	3	2½	2	1¼	1¼	1½	1½	2	1½	1½	1	1
Runner of the Stay	2½	2½	2									
Pennant of the Stay	3	3	2¼	2	1½							
Top-rope	4	3½	3½	2½	2	2	1½					
Parts of the Stay	2	2	1½	1½	1	1	1					1
Pennant for Back-stays	3	2½	2½									
Falls	2½	2	1¼									

The

The Bigness of the Main-top-gallant Rigging.	1 *Mast of 34 Inch.* Inch	2 *Mast of 32 Inch.* Inch	3 *Mast of 30 Inch.* Inch	4 *Mast of 29 Inch.* Inch	5 *Mast of 28 Inch.* Inch	6 *Mast of 27 Inch.* Inch	7 *Mast of 26 Inch.* Inch	8 *Mast of 24 Inch.* Inch	9 *Mast of 23 Inch.* Inch	10 *Mast of 19 Inch.* Inch	11 *Mast of 13 Inch.* Inch	12 *Mast of 12 Inch.* Inch
Pennants of Tackles	3	3	2½	2	2	2	2					1½
Falls of Tackles	2½	2	3¼	3½	3	3	1¾					1½
Shrouds	3	3	3¼	3½	3	3	2¼	2	2	1¼	1½	1
Lanniards	1¼	1½	1½	1½	1½	1½	1	1	1	1	1	1
Puttocks	3½	3	2½	2	2	2	1½	1½	1½	1	1	1
Pennants of Back-stays	3	3	2½	2	2	2						
Falls to them	2	2	1½	1½	1	1						
The Stay	3	3	3	2½	2	2	1½	2	1½	1	1	1
Lanyard	2½	2½	2½	2	2	2	1½	1¼	1¼	1	1	1
Braces	2	1½	1¼	1¼	1¼	1	1	1	1	¼	¼	¼
Pennant of Braces	2½	2½	2	2	1½	1½	1	1	1	1	1	1
Bowlines	2½	2	1¼	1½	1½	1½	1	1	1	¼	¾	¼
Bridles	2	1½	1¼	1¼	1	1	1	1	1	¼	¼	
Top-rope	4½	4	3½	2½	2	2						
Parrel-rope	2½	2	2	2	1¾	1½	1	1½	1	1	1	1
Tye	3	3	3	2½	2½	2	1¾	2½	2	2	1¾	1¼
Halliards	3	2½	2	2	1¼	1½	1	1½	1½	1½	1¼	1¼
Lifts	2½	2	1½	1½	1	1	1	1	1	1	1	1
Flag-Staff-stay	2½	2	1½	1½	1	1						
Cluelines	2	2	1¾	1½	1½	1	1	1½	1½	1¼	1	1

The

Of Rigging a Ship.

The Bigness of the Fore-top-gallant Rigging.

	Mast of 34 Inch.	Mast of 32 Inch.	Mast of 30 Inch.	Mast of 29 Inch.	Mast of 28 Inch.	Mast of 27 Inch.	Mast of 26 Inch.	Mast of 24 Inch.	Mast of 23 Inch.	Mast of 19 Inch.	Mast of 13 Inch.	Mast of 12 Inch.
	1 Inch	2 Inch	3 Inch	4 Inch	5 Inch	6 Inch	7 Inch	8 Inch	9 Inch	10 Inch	11 Inch	12 Inch
Tye	$2\frac{1}{2}$	$2\frac{1}{2}$	$1\frac{3}{4}$	$1\frac{3}{4}$	$1\frac{1}{2}$	$1\frac{1}{2}$	$1\frac{1}{4}$	$2\frac{1}{2}$	2	$1\frac{1}{4}$	$1\frac{1}{4}$	$1\frac{1}{4}$
Halliards	$2\frac{1}{4}$	$1\frac{3}{4}$	$1\frac{1}{2}$	1	1	1	1	$1\frac{1}{2}$	$1\frac{1}{2}$	1	1	1
Bowlines	2	2	$1\frac{1}{2}$	$1\frac{1}{4}$	$1\frac{1}{4}$	$1\frac{1}{4}$	1	1	1	$\frac{1}{4}$		
Bridles	$1\frac{1}{4}$	$1\frac{1}{2}$	$1\frac{1}{2}$	$1\frac{1}{2}$	$1\frac{1}{2}$	$1\frac{1}{4}$	1	1	1	$\frac{1}{4}$		
Stay	$2\frac{1}{2}$	$2\frac{1}{2}$	2	2	$1\frac{1}{4}$	$1\frac{1}{2}$	1	$1\frac{1}{2}$	$1\frac{1}{2}$	1		
Shrouds	$2\frac{1}{2}$	$2\frac{1}{2}$	2	2	$1\frac{1}{2}$	$1\frac{1}{2}$	1	2	$1\frac{1}{2}$	1		
Lanniards	$1\frac{1}{2}$	$1\frac{1}{2}$	$1\frac{1}{2}$	1	1	1	1	$1\frac{1}{4}$	1	$\frac{1}{4}$		
Parrel-rope	2	2	$1\frac{1}{2}$	$1\frac{1}{2}$	1	1	1	$1\frac{1}{2}$	$1\frac{1}{2}$	1		
Cluelines	2	$1\frac{1}{4}$	$1\frac{1}{2}$	$1\frac{1}{2}$	$1\frac{1}{4}$	$1\frac{1}{4}$	1	$1\frac{1}{2}$	$1\frac{1}{2}$	1		
Braces	2	$1\frac{1}{2}$	$1\frac{1}{2}$	$1\frac{1}{4}$	$1\frac{1}{4}$	1	1	1	1	$\frac{1}{4}$		
Lifts	2	$1\frac{1}{4}$	$1\frac{1}{2}$	$1\frac{1}{2}$	$1\frac{1}{4}$	1	1	1	1	1		
Top-rope	$3\frac{1}{2}$	3	3	$2\frac{1}{2}$								
Pennant of Tackles	3	$2\frac{1}{2}$	$1\frac{3}{4}$									
Falls	$2\frac{1}{4}$	2	2									
Puttocks	3	$2\frac{1}{2}$	$2\frac{1}{4}$	2	$1\frac{1}{4}$	$1\frac{1}{2}$	$1\frac{1}{2}$	1	1	1	1	
Back-stays	$2\frac{1}{2}$	$2\frac{1}{2}$	2									

Weight

Of Rigging a Ship.

Weight of Anchors.

1.

            C. q. p. ou.
Sheet Anchor 60 0 0 3
Best Bower   56 0 0 1
Small Bower 55 0 0 0
Stream Anchor 25 0 0 0
Kedg Anchor   0 2 0 2

2.

Sheet Anchor 43 0 0 3
Best Bower   40 0 0 5
Small Bower 39 0 0 3
Stream Anchor 20 0 1 2
Kedg Anchor   7 2 0 0

3.

Sheet Anchor 35 3 3 2
Best Bower   34 0 0 2
Small Bower 31 2 2 7
Stream Anchor 11 3 2 5
Kedg Anchor   4 0 0 2

4.

Sheet Anchor 32 0 0 0
Best Bower   30 0 0 0
Small Bower 27 0 2 2
Stream Anchor 11 0 0 0
Kedg Anchor   3 1 0 0

5.

           C. p. q.
Sheet Anchor 29 0 0
Best Bower   25 0 0
Small Bower 23 3 2
Stream Anchor 9 0 0
Kedg Anchor   2 2 7

6.

Sheet Anchor 28 0 0
Best Bower   27 0 0
Small Bower 16 0 0
Stream Anchor 4 3 2
Kedg Anchor   2 3 0

7.

Sheet Anchor 22 0 2
Best Bower   11 0 0
Small Bower 9½ 0 0
Stream Anchor 5 0 2
Kedg Anchor   2 0 0

8.

Sheet Anchor 27 0 0
Best Bower   23 3 5
Small Bower 23 0 0

9.

           C. q. p.
Sheet Anchor 18 0 0
Best Bower   17 0 0
Small Bower 16 0 2
Stream Anchor 4 2 0
Kedg Anchor   2 2 0

10.

Sheet Anchor 11 0 0
Best Bower   10 0 0
Small Bower   9 0 2

11.

Sheet Anchor 7 0 0
Best Bower   6 0 0
Small Bower   5 2 0

12.

Sheet Anchor 5 0 2
Best Bower   4 0 0
Small Bower   3 2 3

K 2   *Sizes*

Sizes of Cables.

1.

	Inches.
Cables of	21
Cables of	20
Cables of	14½
Cables of	10
Cables of	9

2.

	Inches.
Cables of	20
Cables of	19
Cables of	13
Cables of	9
Cables of	8

3.

	Inches.
Cables of	17
Cables of	16
Cables of	12
Cables of	8

4.

Cables of	17
Cables of	16
Cables of	11

5.

Cables of	15
Cables of	14
Cables of	9

6.

Cables of	13
Cables of	12

7.

Cables of	10
Cables of	9

8.

Cables of	16
Cables of	15
Cables of	10

9.

Cables of	14
Cables of	13
Cables of	12½
Cables of	2
Cables of	8

10.

Cables of	12
Cables of	11

11.

Cables of	8
Cables of	7½
Cables of	6

12.

Cables of	8
Cables of	7
Cables of	6

CHAP

CHAP. XIV.

The Use *of the Cuts* A, B, C *and* D *at the End of the Book.*

HAving made a Scale by which the Length of the Keel, &c. is laid down, as at the Beginning hereof; and allowing that twelve Inches is a Foot, and six Foot, or two Yards, is one Fathom, you may, from the same Scale, take off Fathoms, Yards and Feet, and, by the Help of the Diagonal, Inches too. And having adjusted your Scale to the Model of the Ship, observe the following Directions.

In Figures *B* and *D* you see two Yards, the one hoisted and the other lowered, or a Portlens; the Top-sail-yard also, one hoisted, and the other down upon the Cap, so must you make in all the Models you raise: The Yard a Portlens gives the Length of Top-sail-sheets, and Lifts, and Tye, or Jeers, and Bunt-lines, and Leech-lines, or Hally-yards, measuring from the Hounds to the Deck.

The Yards hoisted gives the Length of Clue lines, Braces, and Clue-garnets, and Tacks, and Sheets, and Bow-lines.

In the small ones, is shewed the Length of the Shrouds and Top-sail Hally-yards with Braces and Lifts; as in the Figure *B*.

In the Figure *A* is shewed how to give a near Estimation, how many Yards of Canvas is in a Main Course. *Note,* When you come in any Ship or Vessel, and desire to know how many Yards of Canvas is in the Main or Fore Course: First, you must know the Depth of your Sail, and the Breadth of the Canvas that the Sail is made of, then take off so much from the Scale as you see the Cloth is in Breadth, and place so many Cloths in the Model on the Main or Fore Yard, the same Depth that the Sail is on, as you see the Main Course in this Figure: After you have so done, then take a Fathom or two off from your Scale, and measure every Cloth up and down as you do the Ropes, and that gives you the Number of Yards.

Likewise here is shewed in this Figure, the way how to place your Garnet and Runner, and Sprit-sail-top-sail, Cranlines and Main-stay, and Fore-stay, to find the true Length of them.

In the Figure C is shewed the way to find the Number of Yards that is in a Main or Fore Top-sail; the same way that you measure one Sail you must measure all.

But this you must observe, That you are to place your middle Cloth first in a Top-sail, and so from thence to each Yard's-arm, that your Gores at the Clue may fall out right.

Likewise it sheweth the Length of Main-top-sail Bow-lines, and so you must do to find the Length of the Fore-top-sail Bow-lines: Draw only a Line from the Top-sail Yard-arm, to the Main-yard-arm, with your Pen or black Lead: Note from the further Yard-arm, that you may take them at the largest Extent, and so your Braces: In like manner, it shews also the Length of Main-bow-line and Main-sheet, and Main-tack and single Garnet.

As for Braces, draw a Line from the Yard-arm to the Place where the Brace should go, you may draw it double if you please, as the Braces go, or you may draw but one single Line, and so take a Fathom off from your Scale, and where it goes double tell two Fathom, and where it goes single tell but one.

And likewise Fore-top-sail-sheets, draw a Line from the Top-sail-yard that is upon the Cap, as you see in the Model D, down to the Yard-arm that is a Portlens, as you see it is from the Fore-top-sail-yard to the Fore-yard, then take one Fathom or two off your Scale, and measure from the Top-sail-yard to the Fore-yard upon the Line that you have drawn, and then from the Fore-yard's-arm to the Mast, and so down to the Fore-castle, and there you have the just Length of your Top-sail-sheets, and it is left to your own Discretion what Stay you will allow: So likewise must you do for your Main-top-sail-sheet, and Fore-top-gallant Clue-lines, and Top-sail Clue-lines, you must do as you see in the Model, and so for any Ropes whatsoever; if you will have them go after your own way, draw a Line with your black Lead where you will have it go, and so measure the Length of it.

But this note, That when you measure the Stays you must measure the Collar first double three or four Fathom, according as you see the Model require it; for as it becomes the Model, so it will become the Ship or Vessel, and you must know that the Collar belongs to the Length of the Stay.

But for the Pennants of Braces, you must measure them first three Fathom or two Fathom, as you see it will become the Model, and there mark the Block, and so measure the Length of the Brace from that.

A CORDAGE TABLE, *shewing how many Fathom, Feet, and Inches of a Rope of any Size under* 14 *Inches makes a Hundred Weight; with the Construction of the Table, and Rules to calculate the Weight of Ropes to any larger Circumference*

I.	*F.*	*F.*	*I.*	*I.*	*F.*	*F.*	*I.*
1	486	0	0	8	7	3	6
¼	313	3	0	¼	7	0	8
½	216	3	0	½	6	4	3
¾	159	3	0	¾	6	2	1
2	121	3	0	9	6	0	0
¼	96	2	0	¼	5	4	0
½	77	3	0	½	5	2	0
¾	65	4	0	¾	5	0	6
3	54	0	0	10	4	5	0
¼	45	5	2	¼	4	4	1
½	39	3	0	½	4	2	2
¾	34	3	9	¾	4	1	8
4	30	1	6	11	4	0	3
¼	26	5	3	¼	3	5	7
½	24	0	0	½	3	4	1
¾	21	3	0	¾	3	3	3
5	19	3	0	12	3	2	3
¼	17	4	0	¼	3	2	1
½	16	1	0	½	3	2	0
¾	14	4	6	¾	2	7	8
6	13	3	0	13	2	5	3
¼	12	2	0	¼	2	4	9
½	11	3	0	½	2	4	0
¾	10	4	0	¾	2	3	6
7	9	5	6	14	2	2	1
¼	9	1	6				
½	8	4	0				
¾	8	3	6				
8	7	3	6				

The Use of the CORDAGE TABLE.

The Letters *I. F. F. I.* at the Top of the Table signify *Inches*, *Fathoms*, *Feet* and *Inches*. The first Column being the Thickness of the Rope in *Inches* and *Quarters*, and the other three the *Fathoms*, *Feet* and *Inches* that make up a hundred Weight of such a Rope. One *Example* will make it plain.

Suppose I desire to know how much of a 7 *Inch* Rope will make a hundred Weight; find 7 in the first Column under *I.* or *Inches* thickness of the Rope, and against that, in the second, third, and fourth Columns, you find 9 | 5 | 6; which shews, that in a Rope of 7 Inches there will be 9 Fathom, 5 Foot, and 6 Inches be required to make a hundred Weight. And so in a 9 Inch Rope, 6 Fathom makes a hundred Weight: And in a three Inch Rope 54 Fathom makes a hundred Weight, &c.

The Construction of this TABLE *is from hence.*

A Rope of 1 Inch about requires 486 Fathom to make up a hundred Weight; and, as the superficial Content of all Circles are in proportion to the Squares of Diameters (and consequently to the Squares of their Circumferences) it will follow, that as a Rope of 1 Inch in Circumference whose Square is also 1, has 486 Fathom to a hundred Weight; 486 divided by the Square of the Circumference, or Girt of any other Rope, the Quotient will give the Number of Fathoms in a hundred Weight. As for *Example*: In a 9 Inch Rope, 9 times 9 is 81, by which divide 486, the Quotient is 6, the Fathoms in a hundred Weight. And so for a 3 Inch Rope, 3 times 3 is 9, by which divide 486, the Quotient is 54 Fathom to a hundred Weight, as in the Table; and where there is a Fraction in the Division, it may be reduced to Feet and Inches; 6 Feet being a Fathom, and 12 Inches a Foot.

A

Of Rigging a Ship.

I.	C.	Q.
3	2	1
3½	3	0
4	4	0
4½	5	0
5	6	1
5½	7	2
6	9	0
6½	10	2
7	12	1
7½	14	0
8	16	0
8½	18	0
9	20	1
9½	22	2
10	25	0
10½	27	2
11	30	1
11½	33	0
12	36	0
12½	39	0
13	42	1
13½	45	2
14	49	0
14½	52	2
15	56	1
15½	60	0
16	64	0
16½	68	0
17	72	1
17½	76	2
18	81	0
18½	85	2
19	90	1
19½	95	0
20	100	0
20½	105	0
21	110	1
21½	115	2
22	121	0
22½	126	2
23	132	1
23½	138	0
24	144	0

A TABLE *shewing the Weight of any Cable or Rope of* 120 *Fathom in Length, and for every half Inch from* 3 *Inches to* 24 *in Circumference.*

I chose to instance in a Cable of the Length above mentioned, because Yarn set at 200 Fathom will, in the laying of a Cable, work up or shorten to 120 Fathom; Cable-laid Ropes working in about two Parts in five; but if it is a half Cable, or a part of a Cable of any other Length, the Weight of 120 Fathom being found by the Table, the Weight of any lesser Part is easily found in proportion to its Length.

Example of the Use of the TABLE.

The first Column marked *I.* for *Inches*, is the Thickness or Circumference of the Cable to every half Inch from 3 to 24; the second and third, marked *C. Q.* for *Hundreds* and *Quarters*, are the Hundreds and Quarters that it will weigh if 120 Fathom in Length. As for Instance, suppose a Cable of fourteen Inches and a half; look against 14½ in the first Column, and you find against it in the other Columns 52 | 2; which shews that 120 Fathom of Cable of 14 Inches and a half about, will weigh 52 Hundred 2 Quarters, or 52 Hundred and a half; and so in others. And any of a lesser Length will weigh in proportion.

The Construction of this Table is from hence, That as all Cables are solid Bodies, and may properly come under the Denomination of Cylinders, and as such the Weight of Cables of any determinate Length will be in proportion to the Squares of their Circumferences. From this Foundation, and my own Experience, I have formed this general brief Rule, viz. *Multiply the Thickness of the Cable by it self, and one fourth of that Product is the Weight of* 120 *Fathom.* As for Instance; suppose a Cable of 12 Inches, 12 times 12 is 144, the Quarter of which is 36, the Weight of 120 Fathom of a Cable of 12 Inches; as you see in the Table.

Note, This Table gives the utmost Weight of Cables of the Length and Size proposed, and something, tho' inconsiderably, differs from the foregoing. As for Instance; in the foregoing Table 6 Fathom of a 9 Inch Rope makes a Hundred Weight, and consequently 120 Fathom should be just 20 hundred Weight, but in this it makes 20 Hundred and 1 Quarter; but the Difference is inconsiderable, and the Cables never exceed the Weight here proposed.

FINIS.

C

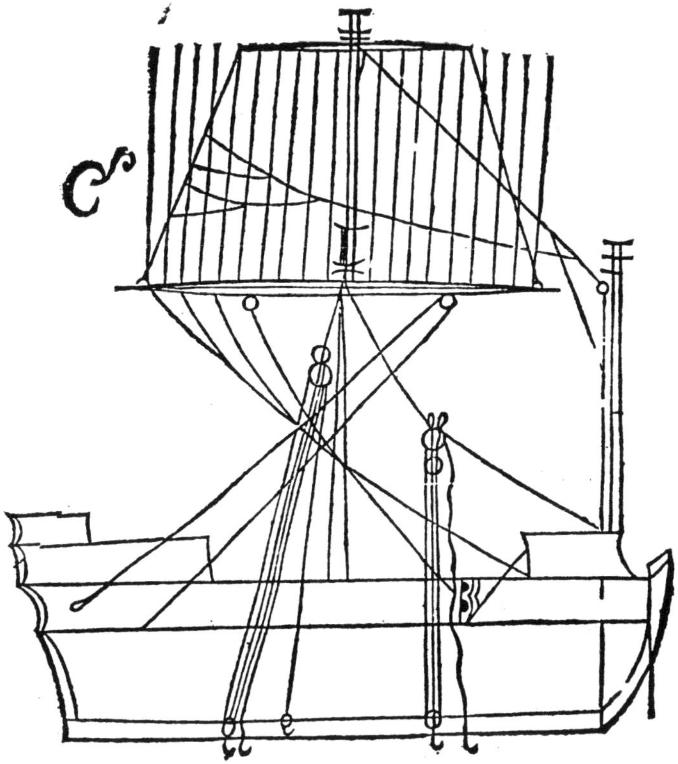

B

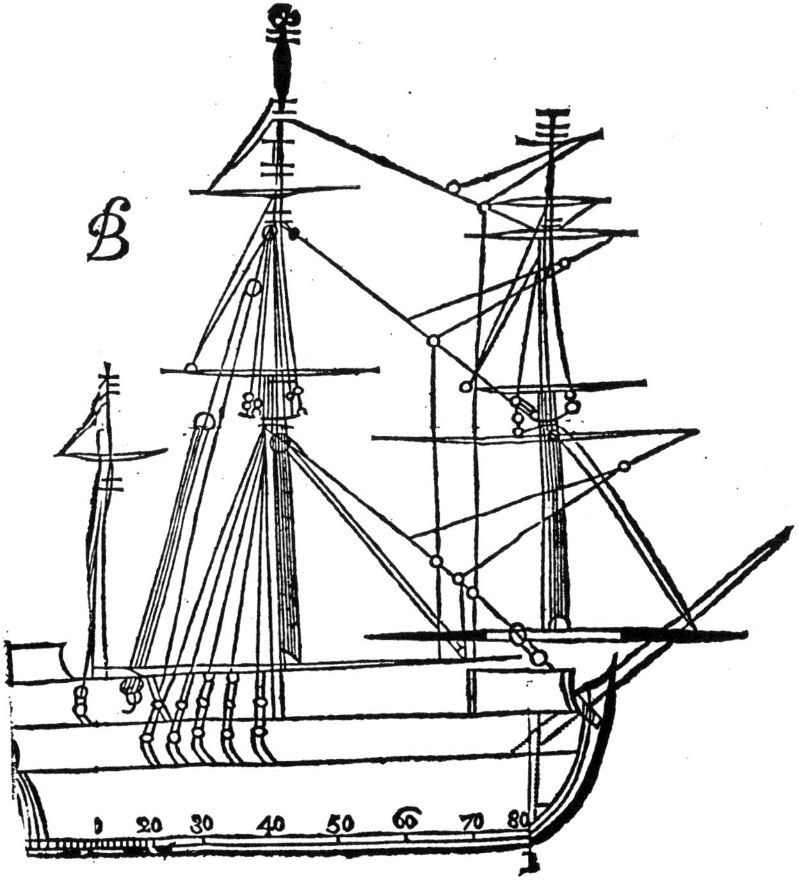

A

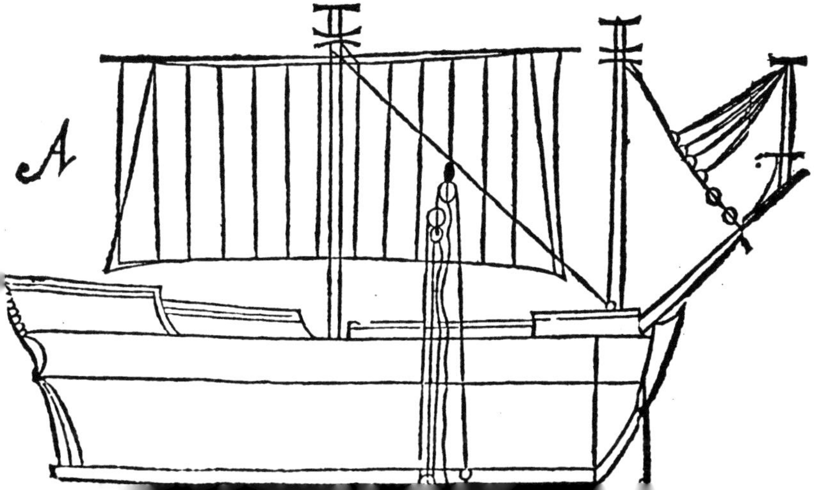

The Figure of the SCALE

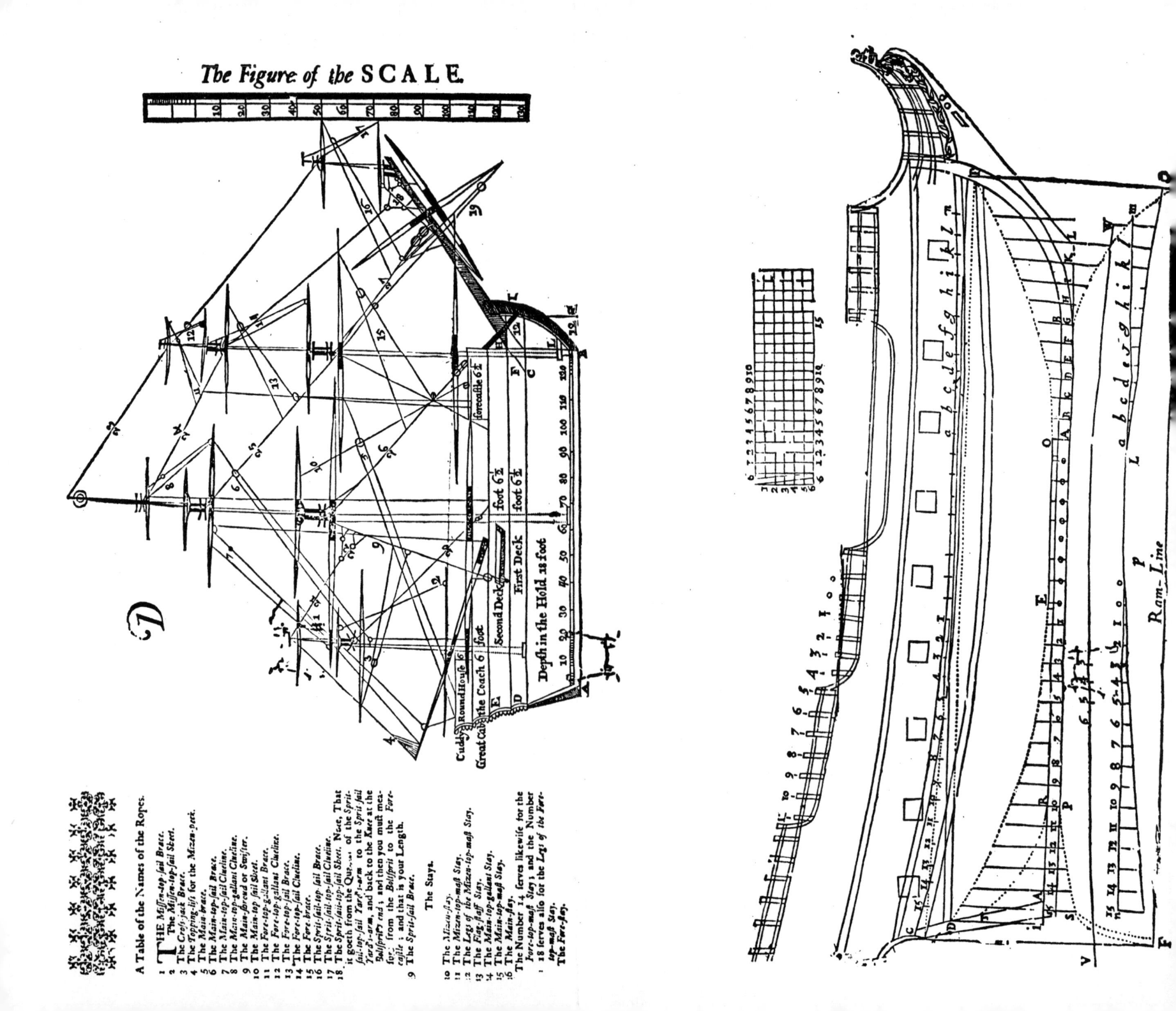

A Table of the Names of the Ropes.

1. THE *Mizzen-top-sail Brace.*
2. The *Mizzen-top-sail Sheet.*
3. The *Cross-jack Brace.*
4. The *Topping-lift for the Mizzen-yard.*
5. The *Main-brace.*
6. The *Main-top-sail Brace.*
7. The *Main-top-gallant Clueline.*
8. The *Main-broad or Swifter.*
9. The *Main-top-sail Sheet.*
10. The *Fore-top-gallant Brace.*
11. The *Fore-top-gallant Clueline.*
12. The *Fore-top-sail Brace.*
13. The *Fore-brace.*
14. The *Fore-top-sail Clueline.*
15. The *Sprit-sail-top-sail Brace.*
16. The *Sprit-sail-top-sail Clueline.*
17. The *Sprit-sail-top-sail Sheet.* Note, That
18. The *Sprit-sail Brace*, it goeth from the Que— of the *Spritsail-top-sail Yard's-arm*, to the *Spritsail Bolsprit's end*, and back to the *Knee* at the *Bolsprit* from the *Forecastle*; and then you must measure for the *Bolsprit* to the *Forecastle*; and that is your Length.
9. The *Spritsail Brace.*

The Stays.

10. The *Mizzen-stay.*
11. The *Mizzen-top-mast Stay.*
12. The *Leg of the Mizzen-top-mast Stay.*
13. The *Flag-staff Stay.*
14. The *Main-top-gallant Stay.*
15. The *Main-top-mast Stay.*
16. The *Main-stay.*

The Number 14 serves likewise for the *Fore-top-mast Stay*; and the Number 18 serves also for the *Leg of the Fore-top-mast Stay.*

The *Fore-stay.*